A Day on the Bay

Going Crabbing,
When the Crab gets out of the basket.

2

A Day on the Bay

Steamer Dreamland at Love Point, Md.

DREAMLAND.

Postcard Views of the Chesapeake

BERT & ANTHEA SMITH

With a Foreword by Jacques Kelly

The Johns Hopkins University Press
Baltimore and London

The Johns Hopkins University Press
2715 North Charles Street
Baltimore, Maryland 21218-4363
www.press.jhu.edu

All postcards in this book are from the collection of
the authors, with the exception of figs. 3, 7, 12, 29, 41,
80, 89, 90, and 164, which appear here with the kind
permission of Roland Forster; and figs. 4, 20, 77, 78, 79,
81, 91, 94, 98, 99, 118, 127, and 132, graciously lent by
Al Bernard.

ISBN 0-8018-6857-2
LC 2001004651

A catalog record for this book is available from the
British Library.

To H. Mebane Turner for his valuable and continuing support

4

CONTENTS

FOREWORD

It was one of those summertime rituals. I was spending the day at my great uncle's shore place off the Log Inn Road, between the Bay Bridge and the mouth of the Magothy River in Anne Arundel County. Sometime after supper we'd stand on his little piece of beach and train our eyes across the water—full of sea nettles of course—and wait for the familiar silhouette of an Old Bay Line boat. These were the last of their kind, not at all like the more numerous freighters and oilers that passed through the channel. The Bay boats were passenger carriers and, at this hour of the evening, were outlined with electric lights. I thought they looked like some sort of bobbing and twinkling German Christmas ornament as they headed down the Bay.

One of the regrets of my life in Baltimore was that I never sailed on the *City of Norfolk.* I missed my chance before the service stopped in 1962. And, worse, I was reminded of my mistake many times over. For years, well in the 1960s, Bay boats sat unused and mothballed in the harbor, waiting for someone to restore them to service and reopen the wharves and resorts where they called.

I inherited my interest in the Bay boats from my father, who grew up in South Baltimore and spent hours in the 1920s and 1930s watching their smokey comings and goings from Federal Hill park. He's often described how energetic they looked, churning their way in and out of the harbor. It was a great free show, those steam engines making those walking beams ride up and down. It was said you could distinguish each boat by its distinctive whistle.

We cherish our rosy recollections of these boats, often forgetting how many were components in a sophisticated transportation network. We think of them as summertime excursion vessels and forget that most earned their way as freight carriers owned by no-nonsense railroad transportation giants. The Chesapeake Bay and its tributaries was an interstate highway system for them.

In the heyday of the summertime steamers, the pages of Baltimore newspapers were filled with small advertisements for the economical day trips they offered. If the destinations were not glamorous, they made up for it in Maryland charm and good cooking. If the Chesapeake's sober little collection of amusement rialtos and bathhouses were no competition for Atlantic City and Coney Island, we liked it that way.

JACQUES KELLY

ACKNOWLEDGMENTS

Our appreciation for the help many people gave us with this, our third postcard book, cannot be overstated. Foremost are the fine old postcards lent by Roland Forster and Al Bernard, both seasoned Bay country collectors and valued friends, without whom this would be a far less interesting volume. Thanks must also go in huge measure to the staff at the Maryland Room of the Enoch Pratt Free Library for their interest and dedication. John and Rosalie Corliss, Dee Delcher and Bernie Franks, George and Marcella Lorden, Sunny and Wade Rice, Neal and Tillie Boyle, and Sally Raynes were once again extremely helpful as dealers and friends, and especially Shirley Stonesifer, who found us pawing through her postcards many times.

At the Johns Hopkins University Press, history editor Robert J. Brugger and regional books marketing manager Jack Holmes encouraged us from the start and kept us on track, and Anne Whitmore improved the manuscript with her careful editing. Bay sailor Tom Finn lent a wonderful book, and Carol Mylander lent us her entire Bay library. As before, photographer Norman Watkins proved a reliable and creative ally, and Eric Agner contributed his immense knowledge and perfect artistry with type. Friends and colleagues at the University of Baltimore understood when patience thinned and deadlines loomed. At almost the last minute, Harvey Bossler filled in some yawning gaps. Thanks also to Gayle Stauffer and her staff at the Cecil Community College Library; Mary Louise de Sarran, librarian at the Maryland Historical Trust; Ken Cawley, archivist and curator of manuscripts at the University of Notre Dame; Heather Maloney, innkeeper at The Oaks; and Brother Tom Morrisy of the Xaverian Brothers in Catonsville.

5

INTRODUCTION

Among my most treasured postcards are those from the clear blue waters and sandy shores of the Chesapeake Bay of long ago. In these favorite cards the sun is always shining, and lucky vacationers are swimming, sailing, and even dancing on the beach. In the years before World War I, proper ladies with parasols promenade along crude wooden boardwalks, and families amble ashore with heavy picnic hampers and children in tow, anticipating an afternoon of shade and cool Bay breezes. The sporty side-wheelers from which they have just disembarked idle in the background, the invisible crew already preparing for the return to Baltimore.

Bearing messages both practical and romantic, these old cards bring back memories of calm summer mornings, exhilarating afternoon sails, peaceful sunsets, and youthful midnight romances. Many are postmarked from towns no longer on the map and dusty landings long abandoned, like those at Mayo, Claiborne, Love Point, and McDaniel. They show the Bay as it was in another age, and a pace of life that has long ago disappeared.

This collection has been assembled to illustrate how we have used the Bay for enjoyment. Postcards, after all, are for tourists and travelers, so very few record the workaday world. Here, then, there are no oystermen on their skipjacks or watermen hauling crab traps; none of the crowded packing houses, crab pickers, or busy canneries of the lower Eastern Shore; no hardscrabble clapboard villages like those on Tangier, Kent, or Smith Islands. I have, however, included some of the many humorous cartoon cards from this earlier era, the ones you would find

6

in any boardwalk souvenir shop, restaurant, or drugstore. They were always located next to the cash register, hard to ignore when paying your bill. Mailed to friends and family back home, they never failed to produce a smile and prove what a great time you were having.

When picture postcards arrived in America, they became fanatically popular; they caused panic in the post office in 1908, but finally emerged as the one souvenir everyone could afford to send or collect by the album-ful. From around

1905, black-and-white photographs were reproduced, some in their original monochrome and others with color overprinted. A great number were carefully tinted by hand, one by one. Today these are especially prized for their sharp detail and documentary quality, as well as for their soft palettes. Later cards were brighter and more colorful, as the 1930s and '40s were overtaken by the Art Deco and Streamline styles. After 1950, though, postcards were simply reproductions of color photos, providing a good record of where you had been but in a way that was not as imaginative or visually interesting as before.

Of course, it is impossible to include every beach, summer camp, and steamboat in a book of this size, but the images here provide a good sample of the hundreds of Bay postcards. Sadly, in our research we found no cards of the African-American resorts, such as Highland Beach, founded by the son of Frederick Douglass, and Carr's Beach. As in my first two books, I have slightly enlarged the cards, to bring out the details in the people, cars, boats, and buildings from the past. So, all aboard with your ticket in hand. Please watch your step on the gangplank—the whistle's about to blow. Hurry up to the top deck, grab a chair, and get ready to enjoy *A Day on the Bay!*

BERT SMITH

8

STEAMER LOUISE, MOONLIGHT ON THE CHESAPEAKE.

Steamer "Dreamland" on the Chesapeake Bay from Baltimore Md.

9

VIEW OF HARBOR, SHOWING EXCURSION BOATS, BALTIMORE, MD.

Steamboats out of Baltimore

Old Bay Line Pier, Baltimore, Md.

THE BALTIMORE STEAM PACKET CO.
LEAVES BALTIMORE EVERY WEEK DAY AT 6.30 P. M.
FOR OLD POINT, NORFOLK AND PORTSMOUTH.

11

In the days before the Chesapeake Bay Bridge and two cars in every garage, families longing for a holiday, be it for one day or several, stepped aboard one of the dozens of steamboats that traveled the waters of the Chesapeake Bay.

On a typical day in June, some chose the steamer *Dreamland,* berthed at the foot of Broadway. For fifty cents each round trip, they enjoyed the three-hour cruise on that huge side-wheeler to Chesapeake Beach. Families and church groups crowded her decks, all eager to leave behind the city's dust and heat. During the return trip, after a day's fun at the beach, couples passed the time dancing to a live orchestra on her large open-air dance floor, whether by moonlight or raindrops, while the *Dreamland* made her way

The Louise (10), often called Baltimore's favorite steamer, returns to the harbor in this view from around 1920. Built in 1864, she carried over five million passengers for the Tolchester Steamboat Company until her end in 1925. On this card from around 1910, the landmark cupola of the Old Bay Line terminal (11) sports a hand-drawn flag. Horses wait patiently along Pratt Street. Amenities aboard the Old Bay Line's brand-new State of Virginia (12) decorate this multiview card postmarked June 6, 1928.

LOUNGE ENTRANCE PALM ROOM

SOCIAL HALL

OLD BAY LINE. Service Since 1840

DINING ROOM

PALM AND MUSIC ROOM

12

home, often racing other steamers sharing her route. The appearance of the Broadway Recreation Pier lights on the horizon signaled that only a dance or two remained. And while the crew secured the *Dreamland* in her berth, trolleys stood waiting to take her sleepy sunburned passengers home, ready to face the coming work week.

An "all-girl orchestra" of three provides the rhythm for a group of well-dressed dancers (13) aboard an Old Bay Line boat in the 1920s. In a card from the same decade that is more painting than photograph, the City of Norfolk *(14) plies the Bay. Not to be outdone, the Merchants and Miners Line offered similar diversions aboard their ships (15), as shown in this card from 1928. The Tolchester Line's* Express *(16) appears newly painted in 1932, while the Wilson Line's two most famous boats, the* Dixie *(17) and the* Bay Belle *(18), sail against blazing sunsets almost a decade later.*

DANCING ON BOARD NEW STEAMERS—BALTIMORE STEAM PACKET CO. (OLD BAY LINE)

STEAMERS "CITY of BALTIMORE" and "CITY of NORFOLK" SISTER SHIPS

Finest Passenger Steamers on the Chesapeake Bay

CHESAPEAKE STEAMSHIP COMPANY—BALTIMORE, MD.

ON SHIPBOARD -- MERCHANTS & MINERS TRANSPORTATION CO.

BOSTON · PROVIDENCE · PHILADELPHIA · BALTIMORE · NORFOLK · NEWPORT NEWS · SAVANN
JACKSONVILLE · WEST PALM BEACH · MIAMI

719-30

STEAMER "EXPRESS", BALTIMORE'S LARGEST EXCURSION STEAMER, BALTIMORE, MD.

107110

Others selected the *President Warfield,* a Merchants and Miners ship, and sailed to Boston, spending a charming night on the Bay, a ten-hour day in Newport News and Norfolk seeing the sights, then two nights and a day at sea before reaching their final destination.

Many a businessman answered the call of the Old Bay Line's brochure to spend his travel time to Norfolk "living in luxury for a golden evening, night, and early morning on the sparkling waters of the Chesapeake Bay," where a world of enjoyment could be packed into those brief hours, "if you care to spend them that way." Passenger cabins ranged from closet-sized cubicles with double-decker berths to spacious rooms with twin beds. Polished brass, ornate stairways, and king-size chairs graced the main salon, while

WILSON LINE STEAMER—S. S. DIXIE

8—S. S. "Bay Belle"

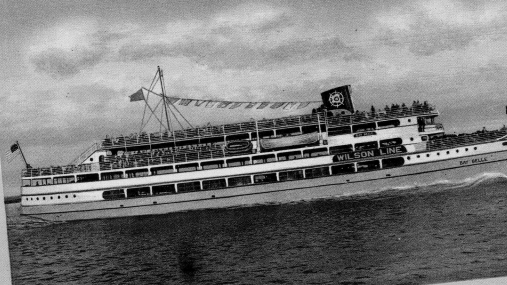

DAY AND MOONLIGHT CRUISES DOWN CHESAPEAKE BAY

Daily Cruises from Baltimore to Betterton, Md.

Ladies in their hats line the rail as the Lord Baltimore (19), an Ericsson steamer, heads to Philadelphia through the C&D Canal at Chesapeake City, Maryland, around 1918.

diners enjoyed white linens, gleaming silver, and attentive, courteous white-jacketed waiters.

Food played an important part on trips, short or long. To prepare for an excursion to Betterton or Tolchester Beach, for example, mothers spent hours the night before frying chicken, making deviled eggs and sandwiches, and baking chocolate cakes, all of which they packed into bulging picnic hampers for the next day's outing. Lunch often began before clearing Sparrows Point. For overnight trips, dining rooms offered such culinary delights as Norfolk spots with corn cakes, crab flakes sautéed with Smithfield ham, broiled bluefish with lemon butter, and milk-fed chicken southern style. Pleasantly full patrons finished off their meals with green apple pie with cheese, chilled melon, or a chocolate sundae.

Couples who wanted to spend a memorable evening together crowded aboard the *Bay Belle,* "the ship that's smoother than a waltz," for a moonlight cruise, or the *Emma Giles* for an evening of dancing to Farson's Band while she sailed to the Choptank River and back.

The outbreak of World War II ended trips with no destination, such as the popular moonlight cruises, and siphoned off many of the vessels for war duty. By 1956 the *Bay Belle* remained the only excursion boat in Baltimore, taking passengers to Tolchester Beach and Betterton until May 1962. The ease and splendor of trips to Norfolk ended on April 12, 1962, with the *City of Norfolk*'s final voyage, reportedly the last overnight steamship run in the nation.

STEAMER CLIO AT FAIR VIEW ON PATAPSCO, BALTIMORE MD.

Will you come to

Fair View

I like your company.

Fair View

Fair View Amusement Park, located on the south shore of Rock Creek, owes its establishment to the sons of George Efford, founder in 1892 of the Rock Creek Steamboat Company, which carried freight and passengers from the foot of Broadway. In the 1920s, brothers Charles and Harry Efford, along with Robert Bottomley, erected Fair View near Fort Smallwood in Anne Arundel County and changed the company's emphasis from freight to excursion travel.

The new park immediately attracted the attention of Sunday school groups with its "no liquor sales" policy. They eagerly crowded aboard steamers such as the *Tred Avon, Kitty Knight,* or *Mohawk* for a day of picnicking on Fair View's long sandy beach. Later in the day, they danced in the pavilion or rode the carousel and swings before packing up for the return trip to Baltimore.

Gas rationing and fuel shortages during World War II drastically curtailed the use of the park and eventually forced it to close. In 1945 the Maryland Yacht Club, led by Commodore Albert W. Rhine, leased and then purchased Fair View. After extensive renovations to the clubhouse, bathhouses, and pier, the yacht club used the park as the center of summer activities for its members.

The crew and passengers of the Clio (20) pose on a calm day, probably in 1908, its first season for the Rock Creek Steamboat Company, although it had been built thirty years earlier. This typical "romance" card (21) has the location added neatly by hand and bears an innocent message and a 1917 postmark.

7

21

Bay Shore Park

In the summer of 1906 on land known as Black Marsh, south of North Point, officials of the United Railway and Electric Company cut the ribbon to open the impressive Bay Shore Park. Giuseppe Aiala led the Royal Artillery Band, well known at River View Park, as first-day visitors poured onto the grounds. Baltimore residents looking for recreation and relaxation reached the park via trolley or a short ferry ride. Visitors from across the Bay gained access in 1920 when the Baltimore and Eastern Shore Ferry Line began service from Rock Hall. Arriving vessels docked at the thousand-foot-long concrete pier, discharging their eager passengers, ready for a day of fun surrounded by beautiful gardens and elegant Edwardian architecture at one of the most enjoyable family outing places on the Bay.

Patrons filled countless hours riding the Thing-A-Ma-Jig roller coaster, the Skooter bumper cars, the Toboggan Water Slide, and the Monkey Shine trolley. Visitors who felt more adventurous took boat rides to a lighthouse three miles out in the Bay. Others tried their skill at knocking down the pins in the park's bowling alley. When they grew hungry, families sat down to delicious seafood suppers in the Colonial Dining Room, then they topped off the day by listening to music at the bandstand.

When the park opened for the 1939 season, visitors found the newly completed Crystal Spray pier and real old-style Maryland dinners in the redecorated hotel. The addition of dramatic new lighting allowed nighttime bathing and fun on the amusement rides. Name bands visited several times a season to play for an

Excursion Crowd at Car Station, Bay Shore Park, near Baltimore, Md.

22

23

Carousel, Bay Shore Park, near Baltimore, Md.

evening of dancing in the Florentine Ballroom, overlooking the Bay.

In the 1940 season, ads in the *Sun* touted performances by a complete animal circus as well as "the racer dip, claimed to be one of the longest and fastest rides in the country."

All the fun ended in 1947 when Bethlehem Steel bought the property and dismantled the park. Its remains, purchased in 1987, now form part of North Point State Park, where the trolley station, restaurant, pier, and fountain have been restored.

24

25

The Pier at Bay Shore, (on the Chesapeake,) near Baltimore, Md.

On a warm summer day in 1915, the railroad station at Bay Shore Park (22) overflows with families and school and church groups from Baltimore and as far away as Philadelphia. The carousel (23) offers rides for both children and adults in this view from two years earlier. Featuring complete seafood suppers for 75 cents, the Colonial Dining Room (24) stands ready for the crowds, while the famous Thing-A-Ma-Jig roller coaster waits in the background. Only a few vacationers braved the sun and the pier when this picture was taken (25).

EMMA GILES AT TOLCHESTER WHARF, ANNAPOLIS, MD.

26

27

Annapolis from Eastport, Md.

28

ANNAPOLIS, Md.   View from Capitol Dome toward Eastport.

Hand-colored

Annapolis

Located at the mouth of the Severn River over-looking the waters of the Chesapeake Bay, Maryland's capital enjoys one of the most picturesque settings of any city in America, a setting that impressed John Smith during his explorations in 1608. He wrote of the area: "Here are mountains, hils, valleys, rivers and brooks, all running most pleasantly into a faire Bay, compassed with a fruitful and delightsome land; heaven and earth never agreed better to frame a place for human habitation." Ever since its founding in 1649 by Puritan exiles from Virginia, the "little city on the Severn" has attracted visitors from far and wide to delve into the early history of the nation or to ride the waters of the nearby Bay.

In the past, visitors from Baltimore often boarded steamers such as the *Emma Giles* for a day of sightseeing in Annapolis. Three times a week from 1887 to 1936 the *Emma Giles* transported passengers to a different era when she docked at Annapolis, where more colonial buildings survive than in any other city in America. Travelers from the Eastern Shore took one of the ferries from Claiborne. For travelers continuing north or south, the Claiborne-Annapolis Ferry Company urged motorists to bring their cars aboard, "save 100 miles and avoid the city's congestion." Upon arriving at the city's dock, visitors

Passengers board the already crowded Emma Giles *(26) for a trip up to Tolchester Beach in 1924. Named for and christened by the 5-year-old daughter of a Tolchester Line stockholder in 1887, the side-wheeler carried hundreds of thousands of travelers up and down the Bay until 1936, when she was sold and hauled to Curtis Bay. Set afire in 1959, her end came the same year that 77-year-old Emma Giles Parker died. The Naval Academy's Bancroft Hall and chapel dome are easily identified in this clear photograph of the waterfront (27) in about 1908. "Bird's-eye views" such as this delicately hand-colored card (28) were popular in the years following the Wright brothers' first flight.*

11

could purchase deviled crabcakes from Old Annie, or stop at Middleton Tavern or Shiplap House for some refreshment and the day's news.

History, exuding from very pore of the city, greeted visitors staying for a day or a week, presenting the opportunity to look at the remnants of the early life of the nation. In a 1928 *Sun* article Dr. Gilbert Grosvenor, president of the National Geographic Society, expressed the view of many when he wrote: "Annapolis has been preserved as our country's most truly Colonial city. You may wander this fine old community and feel that you are living in those dramatic days when the little city on the Severn had a major part in shaping the course of the nation's history."

Favorite sites to visit included the State House, the Old Treasury Building, and the Hammond-Harwood House. One of the chief points of interest was the Naval Academy, founded in 1845 by George Bancroft, secretary of the navy under President Polk. It is small wonder that Bancroft selected Annapolis, given its natural harbor, regarded by many as the best natural harbor on the East Coast. Together with the existence of the stone-walled Fort Severn, the harbor gave Annapolis what the Navy needed as a location for its training school for future naval officers. Since 1845 generations of midshipmen have learned the skills necessary for commanding ships at sea. While training them, the Naval Academy has provided entertainment for the millions of visitors to Annapolis, from visits to the chapel, with its crypt containing the remains of naval hero John Paul Jones, to the afternoon formations on the Academy's parade grounds.

The very features that attracted the Naval Academy have also lured boaters to the area. One

THE LAST FAREWELLS, EMBARKING FOR SUMMER'S CRUISE, U. S. NAVAL ACADEMY, ANNAPOLIS, MD.

Dress Parade, U. S. Naval Academy, Annapolis, Md.

1A3129-N

Midshipmen Preparing for Sailboat Drill, U. S. Naval Academy, Annapolis, Md.

OFFICIAL U. S. NAVY PHOTOGRAPH

1B-H2267

Midshipmen Sailboat Drill, U. S. Naval Academy, showing Severn River Bridge, Annapolis, Md.

OFFICIAL U. S. NAVY PHOTOGRAPH

1B-H2268

of the earliest clubs promoting pleasure boating in the area formed in 1885 as the Severn Boat Club. From their clubhouse on Proctors Point at the entrance to Spa Creek, members helped expand the growing interest in boating and yachting until 1937, when burgeoning membership prompted an upgrade in the name to the Annapolis Yacht Club. Operating from a new clubhouse on the original site, the club continued to grow into a well-respected organization. In 1939 the Annapolis Yacht Club held its first ocean race, enticing some of the finest, fastest yachts on the East Coast for the New London, Connecticut, to Annapolis race. That same year the club's regatta tallied a record 238 entries. World War II interrupted the activities but not the interest, and in 1947, with the cooperation of the Naval Academy, the Annapolis Yacht Club, and the New York Yacht Club, an ocean race from Newport, Rhode Island, to Annapolis once again attracted many of the finest racers on the East Coast.

One of the best builders of handcrafted yachts on the East Coast moved to Spa Creek in 1947 from Camden, New Jersey, when the polluted waters of the Delaware River began turning the white hulls of his vessels an unsightly grey. John Trumpy brought his knowledge, skill, and love of wooden ship building to Annapolis and, until his firm closed in 1973,

Midshipmen (29) stage their gear and prepare to embark for the Academy's traditional summer cruise in 1912 under the admiring gaze of family and friends. In the 1920s, companies in full dress and under arms pass in review (30), probably during a June Week parade. The blue stripe on their hat bands identifies these midshipmen (31) as first-year students, or plebes, here getting hands-on knowledge of the basics of seamanship. This linen card is from 1941. Once under way (32), the boats respond to age-old commands, and midshipmen begin to become sailors.

CARVEL HALL HOTEL, ANNAPOLIS, MD.

built some of the finest yachts on the East Coast, including *Williamsburg* for President Harry Truman and *The Sequoia* for Presidents Johnson and Nixon. Because of their shallow draw, these craft easily made the passage south to Florida on the inland route, helping to make Annapolis the yachting capital of the inland waterway.

A 1939 brochure inviting people to visit Annapolis summed up the town's appeal with words that continue to ring true today: "Why go to Florida, California or other faraway places when close at hand is the real land of promise? The Chesapeake Bay country! One hour from Washington or Baltimore brings you to Old Annapolis, the 'Heart of Maryland' and the blue Chesapeake, where land and water meet. A modern city with a Colonial setting."

GENERAL VIEW OF HARBOR AND U. S. NAVAL ACADEMY, BY NIGHT, ANNAPOLIS, MD.

A sporty yellow roadster and its three occupants wait in front of Carvel Hall (33), the popular 200-room hotel favored by midshipmen as a respectable repository for their out-of-town guests and dates. A handwritten note on the back of this card records that rates were $5 a day, or $25 a week, American plan, in November 1928. Today this building, built by William Paca, signer of the Declaration of Independence and an early governor, is one of the most impressive of the many restored eighteenth-century mansions in Annapolis. A waterfront view (34) from about the same time has a perfectly centered full moon and shows every single window of all the Academy buildings, as if all the lights were on, an artistic device that adds visual interest to the view.

Bay Ridge

"Your Waikiki on the Chesapeake," or so says a brochure for Bay Ridge Beach, located on Tolly's Point at the mouth of the Severn River near Annapolis. In its heyday years of the 1880s and 1890s, the steamers *Theodore Weems* and *Louise* each made three trips a day from Baltimore, bringing visitors to this popular 150-acre Bay resort. Others came via the Baltimore & Ohio Railroad's excursions from Philadelphia, which deposited them at Canton for the steamer trip down the Bay.

When they arrived at Bay Ridge, they found a first-class hotel with meals "at city prices," afternoon and evening concerts by the Naval Academy Band, and entertainment that included a troupe of trick cyclists and a death-defying high-diver who reportedly leapt from a 75-foot tower

35

The Baur House and Beach

Bay Ridge, Md. on Chesapeake Bay

36

into a small tank of water. Children delighted in riding the numerous swings and the merry-go-round with the flying horses. Because of its high elevation, Bay Ridge further rewarded its patrons with spectacular views not only of the water but of the dome of the State House, various church spires, and other notable sites of Annapolis.

In 1942, the rigors of World War II pressed Bay Ridge into service as a haven of rest and recuperation for torpedoed sailors.

Two-piece wool bathing suits are still proper for both sexes in this skillfully hand-colored card (35) from the 1920s. Twenty years later, the beach has sprouted a dozen or more thatched Tiki huts (36) and bathing attire is much more colorful and revealing.

BA-H227

Camp Whippoorwill

"Tall pines loom dark o'er the campfire,
The Magothy River is misty and blue,
Moonlight steals over the water
And Camp Whippoorwill—we're singing to you."

For more than seven decades, similar refrains have echoed around the campfires of Camp Whippoorwill, a Girl Scout camp on the Magothy River near Pasadena, dedicated to the joys of waterfront activities and living outdoors. In 1928, under the leadership of Miss Caroline Lyder and armed with a capital fund of only $15,000, the Girl Scouts purchased nineteen acres of forested property from Claude B. Whitby, who had turned the grounds of Susquehanna chief, White Eagle, into Whippoorwill Hill, a camp for boys. By 1935 the camp boasted a new lodge, infirmary, and dock.

In the early years, girls lived in old Army tents with wooden floors and carried drinking water from a spring. By 1932 the addition of a well brought water to the "Big House," or main building; a 1949 water system replaced that well and residents enjoyed hot showers at the end of a long day. A devastating fire in 1939 destroyed the Big House, but the scouts rallied to the cause, selling thousands of boxes of cookies to raise funds to build a new Big House, still in use today.

On a typical day at camp, woodsmoke filled the air as girls twisted biscuit dough around a stick or skewered hot dogs and marshmallows and roasted them over the crackling fire. In craft classes the scouts fashioned pottery from local clay, tooled patterns onto leather belts, or decorated sit-upons with their own individual designs. With its emphasis on water activities, the camp provided the ideal place to learn to swim and canoe.

37

38

A COOK-OUT, CAMP WHIPPOORWILL, PASADENA, MD.

39

Fashions of the 1920s dictated bloomers, middie blouses with black ties, knee stockings with low-heeled shoes, but no long pants. When taking to the water, girls wore two-piece swimsuits made of wool. A 1934 instruction guide noted that campers could receive no candy or food of any kind from home.

In the early years, seventy-five or more girls attended each of the two-week sessions, divided into three units: Peter Pan for the youngest girls (ages 10–11), Sherwood Forest for the intermediate girls (ages 12–13), and Treasure Island for the senior girls (ages 14–18). Comradeships formed, especially around the end-of-day campfires, where girls sang songs, told stories, and made plans before taps sent them off to bed.

The totem pole crafted by two scouts in the 1930s may have disappeared, but the delights of time spent at camp remain as Camp Whippoorwill continues to welcome the Girl Scouts of Central Maryland for days of summer fun on the shores of the Magothy River, just off the Chesapeake Bay.

SAILING — CAMP WHIPPOORWILL

The theatrics and body language of the young speaker hold her fellow Girl Scout campers' attention (37) in this sepia card from about 1940. During an afternoon rest period, tent sides are rolled up (38) while girls chat or write a letter home. A scout leader stirs the pot (39) and the Magothy River provides excellent sailing (40) in these views from the same period.

40

Beverley Beach

One of many summer colonies along the Chesapeake Bay, Beverley Beach owes its existence to Edgar J. Kalb, an entrepreneur who purchased the beachfront and surrounding forests in 1925. Located on the Rhode River, this privately developed, gated resort limited admission to persons on its guest list, namely "gentiles of North European ancestry." From late May to mid-September, people arrived from Baltimore, Annapolis, and Washington; but, instead of staying at a hotel, visitors for more than a day either rented furnished cottages by the week or purchased a homesite in the community.

The 2,300-foot-long Bay beach of clean white sand featured a safe and gradually sloping sandy bottom that allowed even small children to paddle there unattended. In addition to a pleasure boat harbor in Cadles Creek, owner Kalb provided a bathhouse suitable for 4,000 people, complete with a modern gym, large floats, water slides, and illumination for bathing until 11 P.M. A large steel net erected around fourteen acres of bathing area each season protected bathers from bothersome nettles. Picnickers spread their meals on any of the 500 tables beneath the shade of brightly colored umbrellas.

A large hall provided other entertainment. On weekend evenings couples danced to the music of a seven-piece band. A game room lined with "coin-operated devices" allowed others to while away their time feeding coins into the ever-hungry slot machines and other mechanical games. In later years these gaming devices grew more popular and overshadowed the desire for dancing, eventually filling the hall with the never-ending clink of coins in their slots.

The opening of the Chesapeake Bay Bridge in 1952 may have diverted some of the sun wor-

C-1208

REFRESHING

© CURT TEICH & CO., INC.

shipers to the broader, whiter beaches of Ocean City, but the attraction of Beverley Beach remained, owing to the various monetary distractions, until 1968, when the Anne Arundel County Council outlawed slot machines. Mr. Kalb sold his land to a developer in 1972.

Actually a generic design over which the name of any beach could be imprinted (41), this linen card is dated 1939. The swings seem a popular meeting place (42) in this multiview card from the same period. An airbrushed "pin-up girl" (43) decorates this view, postmarked from nearby Mayo on June 24, 1940, and advertising "Dancing every night, music by Jimmie Elliott's Orchestra."

44

Pavilion, Pier and Crab House   North Beach, Md.

SEA FOOD

North Beach

A few miles east of Mount Harmony in northern Calvert County lies the year-round residential community of North Beach. Its origins date to 1910, when the town was developed for employees and patrons of Chesapeake Beach, one mile to the south. In the early days, visitors arriving by train from Washington, D.C., traveled the final mile to their summer cottages in a horse-drawn bus driven by Philip Chew. Later two businessmen built an electric railway, powered by a wood-burning plant. When that proved impractical, a tractor began pulling the car to its final destination.

Sunbathers in all stages of tanning, from white to nut-brown, relax on the sand sometime in the 1940s (44).

The Board Walk, Chesapeake Beach, Md.

45

Visitors at Chesapeake Beach, Md.

Chesapeake Beach

In the late 1890s Colorado railroad builder Otto Mears and Denver banker David Holliday Moffat decided to invest their money in an amusement park and resort on the shores of the Chesapeake Bay. They built not only the resort Chesapeake Beach but also the Chesapeake Railway to bring visitors from the Washington, D.C., area. For a round-trip fare of a quarter, this 28-mile-long line, known as the Honeysuckle Route, brought day-trippers laden with picnic baskets to what its developers hoped would become the "Monte Carlo of the East Coast." In peak season six trains a day made the run, often forcing the railway, affec-tionately referred to as "the old cinder burner," to borrow passenger cars from the B&O Railroad in order to handle the crowds.

Travelers from Baltimore and Philadelphia arrived on the steamer *Dreamland.* From the end of the half-mile-long pier a miniature train took them to shore, where they made a mad dash to claim tables under the oak trees before enjoying the pleasures of the huge casino and the rambling boardwalk with its band shell, dance pavilion, and carousel. Overnight guests stayed at the Belvedere Hotel and later at the Highview. Originally the attractions included a racetrack, but the burrowing habits of muskrats took their toll on it, causing seri-

"Good crabbing, poor bathing, fair dinners, and pretty girls are found here" writes the sender of this card (45), postmarked from Chesapeake Beach on June 15, 1912. Passengers crowd onto the pier as a steamer, probably the Dreamland (46), empties its human cargo once again. Arriving from D.C., a trainload of sun-seekers (47) parades from the station, bathing suits, lunches, and parasols in hand, in this card from the World War I years.

47

Just Arrived at Chesapeake Beach, Md.

Crabbing and Fishing on the Long Pier, Chesapeake Beach, Md.

"Just a Company", Chesapeake Beach, Md.

ous injuries to the horses and forcing the racetrack to close after only two seasons.

Some people chose to crab off the pier, then had their day's catch steamed on site for 35 cents or wrapped in burlap bags for the journey home. Children climbed aboard the Gustav Dentzel carousel or rode the roller coaster, daringly constructed out over the water. Couples danced the evening away to the music of a live orchestra or tested their luck in the gambling casino.

Despite the grand plans for its success, Chesapeake Beach was collapsing into bankruptcy in the late 1920s when new owners resurrected it as Seaside Park with a new ballroom, a saltwater pool, and new rides. From 1931 to 1935 the Wilson Line's steamer *State of Delaware* sailed from Pier 8 Light Street, followed during 1936–41 by the *Dixie* and then by the *Bay Belle*. Steamer service never returned after war restrictions ended it in 1942. The railway made its last trip on April 15, 1935; a short time later the tracks were pulled up and sold for scrap, permanently ending rail service to the resort.

After World War II, Wesley Stinnett bought the park, known once again as Chesapeake Beach, and attempted to reshape it for the growing automobile crowd. The wartime dredging of Fishing Creek allowed for a small harbor and a fleet of twenty-six fishing boats for excursions on the Bay.

In the 1950s and 1960s Chesapeake Beach sported 600 slot machines, which brought new interest to the resort, but that all ended in July 1968 when the state legislature outlawed the gaming devices. The amusement park finally closed in 1972.

Catching the Blues, Solomons, Md.

37264

Fishing Boats, Solomons, Md.

3B-H277

Solomons

Located on the southernmost tip of Calvert County, Solomons Island has long ranked as an excellent fishing ground and a favorite port of call for yachts. Its earlier names include Bourne's Island, Somervell's Island, and Sandy Island, but Solomons Island became official in 1870, several years after Baltimore businessman, Isaac Solomon, chose it for his oyster canning business. Indeed, much of the island consists of oyster shells deposited by those canneries.

In the nineteenth century Solomons, with its excellent harbor and richly stocked waters, quickly became a center for boatbuilding and fishing. Early visitors stayed at Rekkar's Hotel and Bowen's Inn and shopped for supplies at J. C. Webster's store. Steamboats arrived from Baltimore two or three times a week, providing one of the few regular connections with the outside world. Sport fishermen up and down the Bay knew of its value and made their way from Baltimore and the Eastern Shore to fish the waters, helping it develop as a summer resort in the early 1900s. Local homes provided accommodations for tourists, and watermen chartered their boats to fish the waters for the plentiful rockfish.

On summer days people sat under cool trees, went swimming and sailing, or played on the island's baseball teams. For many years Solomons provided

A youth in knickers (48) is caught enjoying some fishing with the adults on a bright afternoon in 1909. Apparently families provided their own makeshift shelters (49) on Chesapeake Beach's camping grounds at about the same time.

An afternoon's catch (50) is proudly displayed in this exuberantly colored card from the 1920s. The fine marina and boat dock are empty of human activity in this linen card (51) postmarked 1947.

winter quarters for the *James Adams Floating Theater Show Boat.* When people heard the band play and the ballyhooers yell each spring and fall, they flocked to the dock to see the troupe perform.

In the 1920s, with the economy in decline, M. M. Davis and other builders of workboats turned their attention to producing custom yachts and pleasure boats. Because of its geographical location, the island became a natural stop for long-distance cruisers headed north and south.

The Great Depression dealt a harsh blow to Solomons, but the storm of August 23, 1933, devastated the island, severely damaging oyster beds, canning plants, packing houses, the steamboat wharf, and boats. In 1937, as interest in the water revived, area yachtsmen formed the Solomons Island Yacht Club; they held its first series of races in August of that year.

New attention arrived with World War II, when the Navy established three bases at the mouth of the Patuxent River. Thousands of military personnel and their families flooded onto the island. Young Marines practiced their amphibious maneuvers before traveling half a world away to the waters of the Pacific Ocean. But the watermen suffered immensely from the lack of access to their customary fishing grounds.

The end of the war brought an end to isolation, and attention quickly turned to development of water-related tourism, introducing new generations to the enjoyable qualities of life in this formerly hardscrabble town.

The artist added the flag (52), an expression of wartime patriotism, to this linen view from 1943. Red lawn chairs and a nautical decor perk up a multiview card (53) of two years earlier.

52

Evans Moving Picture and Amusement Pier, Solomons, Md.

53

DIVING PRACTICE, CAMP CALVERT, LEONARDTOWN, MARYLAND

CANOEING ON BRETON BAY, CAMP CALVERT, LEONARDTOWN, MARYLAND
SUMMER PARADISE FOR BOYS

Camp Calvert

"Every Brother counselor should remember that campers have reached or soon will reach that 'uncertain' period in life—adolescence— when they most need training in the virtues necessary for a Catholic."

Thus began the list of tips to staff members at Camp Calvert on Breton Bay, "the summer paradise for boys" operated from 1917 to 1969 by the Xaverian Brothers from Leonard Hall Academy, located near Leonardtown in St. Mary's County. Ranging in age from 8 to 14, as many as 140 boys attended each of the two four-week sessions. To take advantage of their charges' naturally competitive spirits, the brothers designed activity programs to keep the boys as highly interested as possible, so their participation would be a continuous challenge rather than a mere whiling away of their time at camp.

Sports functioned in the form of leagues for the first three weeks of each session, culminating in tournaments in the final week. At the end of each of the two sessions, trophies were awarded for swimming, tennis, track, and boxing. Other activities included softball, touch football, volleyball, horseback riding, tennis, badminton, archery, and quoits, a game similar to horseshoes using a rope or ring of flattened metal.

The final tip to staff members urged them to retain a sense of humor and the courage to do what they felt was right and reminded them that "a boy never forgets a teacher who has really done his job."

Divers show off their skills in front of other campers and the lifeguard (54) sometime in the 1940s. In another card from the same time, canoes bearing the camp's double-c logo are paddled on the Potomac (55).

Some Shore Humor

Reflecting tastes and themes from another era, these cards are but a sampling of the vast selection of postcards displayed at Bay resorts in the middle of the twentieth century. They celebrate the adventures of fishing and meeting a Bay crab up close, and they bear postmarks from various locations from 1941 to 1961.

THE WAY WE CATCH THEM HERE

Greetings from TILGHMAN, MD.

59

Havre de Grace

The beauty of this part of Maryland so moved General Lafayette in 1782, when he saw it from a ferry crossing the Susquehanna River, that he exclaimed that it was much like Le Havre in his native France and could well be called Le Havre de Grace (Harbor of Mercy). Although the town was known as Susquehanna Lower Ferry, residents quickly adopted the unofficial but very lovely name Havre de Grace. In 1785 the act of the General Assembly incorporating the town made the name official.

Beginning with John Smith's landing in the early seventeenth century, visitors with a high regard for natural beauty and the rewards it offers have trekked to the western shore of the Susquehanna at the top of the Chesapeake Bay. The journey was not without danger, however, because the very conditions that brought large numbers of fish and waterfowl also presented a challenge to safe passage for boaters, namely, the turbulent waters off Concord Point, where the Susquehanna River flows south and meets the tidal flow of the Bay.

Havre de Grace benefited from land and sea travel, being at the site of two railroad lines (the B&O and the Pennsylvania) as well as being a link on the Post Road running north and south. Steamers brought visitors to the area on a regular basis, but the railroads' influence and use overtook the need for the steamers, and regular service ended in 1900 when the *City Belle* burned in the harbor. Attention turned more to pleasure boating, and over the ensuing years this led Havre de Grace to promote itself as the "water sports capital of the Upper Chesapeake Bay."

62

POINT CONCORD LIGHT HOUSE, BY NIGHT, HAVRE DE GRACE, MD.

63

The Outlet Lock of the Old Tide-Water Canal, Havre de Grace, Md.

DUCK SHOOTING AT HAVRE-DE-GRACE, MD.

HOTEL BAYOU, HAVRE DE GRACE, MD.   FINEST HOTEL ON CHESAPEAKE BAY.
60 ROOMS.   WM. PINKNEY WEST, Manager.   MODERN.   FIREPROOF.   60 BATHS.   94541

Abundant fishing immediately drew sportsmen, who found they could choose between swiftly moving currents or gently flowing glassy waters in their pursuit of shad, bass, perch, herring, and bluefish. The Susquehanna Flats, located only a few hundred yards from downtown, and the secluded coves of the area offered them an angler's paradise. To the delight of hunters, the Flats attracted thousands of Canada geese, canvasbacks, mallards, and other waterfowl each season.

In 1912 patrons of thoroughbred horseracing flocked to Havre de Grace Racetrack, one of four mile-long tracks in Maryland (Bowie, Laurel, and Pimlico being the others). Racing fans quickly regarded the oval, with its grandstand facing the Chesapeake Bay, as one of the best racetracks in the country. Legendary horses such as Man o' War, War Admiral, and Citation raced there. Having survived the Great Depression and World War II, the track finally closed in 1951 following the death of Edward Burke, one of its founders and the "heart" of the track.

In the years before World War II, Havre de Grace developed into a regional recreation center, offering fine modern hotels and the cuisine that has made Maryland tables famous from colonial times. The area that so impressed Lafayette continues to lure people to venture north to the top of the Bay.

A full moon illuminates the scene as a powerful lighthouse beam (62) warns passing vessels in this imaginatively printed card from the 1920s. A completely different mood is captured with warmer colors in this detailed view (63) from before World War I. The now-outlawed practice of shooting ducks from a sinkbox in which the hunter could lie down below the water line with his double-barrelled 4-guage gun is demonstrated here (64) in a view postmarked from nearby Perryville in 1925. The Hotel Bayou advertises "Racing, Fishing, Boating, Gunning," and an indoor pool, among other amenities, on the back of this card (65) mailed in 1928.

North East

Located at the very top of the Bay, the town of North East, founded in 1658, takes its name from the nearby Northeast River. Initially the community supported itself with woolen and flour mills, a brick kiln, and an iron foundry. Out-of-town shipping included wood products, grain, produce, and tobacco. Among those attracted to North East were master basketmakers Edward and Samuel Day of Massachusetts, who arrived in 1876 to continue manufacturing and supplying white oak baskets to the southern market. By World War I their factory was producing 2,000 baskets each week, and it continues to make them as it has done for more than a hundred years.

Unfortunately, the Northeast River lacked sufficient depth to operate as a major port, and by 1910 much of the shipping business had shifted east to the more navigable Elk River, so activity on the water focused instead on year-round recreation, attracting people from nearby states and the lower Bay for fishing, hunting, and pleasure boating. Rockfish, large-mouth bass, and white and yellow perch kept fisherman on their toes, while the ducks and geese that flocked to the area in autumn provided hunters with ample targets to test their shooting skills. In winter the hardiest outdoorsmen returned for ice fishing.

Although plans for Turkey Point Lighthouse date to as early as 1812, construction on the 35-foot masonry tower actually began in 1832. Completed in 1833, the lighthouse sits atop a bluff

Back when boats were still crafted of wood, this sleek little powerboat (66) skips across a calm bit of water in the 1940s. At the very top of the Bay, picnickers (67) enjoy a summer outing as a trim sailboat passes by in this card from the same time.

RED POINT BEACH, NORTH EAST, MD.

67

RED POINT BEACH, NORTH EAST, MD.

6—McDaniels Yacht Basin on North East River, Gateway to Chesapeake Bay, North East, Md.

1B-H2172

7—Pier at Bay Boat Works, Hances Point near North East, Md.

1B-H2173

100 feet above the Bay where the Northeast and Elk Rivers meet. The original light used three brass oil lamps, which had to be cleaned and filled every day. Electrification arrived in 1943. Automation in 1948 ended the need for a resident keeper, so Fanny Mae Salter, serving since 1925, retired. Solar power now fuels the light as it continues to guide vessels headed for the nearby Chesapeake and Delaware Canal.

One of the biggest attractions to the upper Bay began in 1936 when the state was bequeathed a 368-acre estate, providing the foundation for Elk Neck State Park, the first state park on the shores of the Chesapeake Bay. In May 1937 members of the Civilian Conservation Corps constructed cabins, trails, bathhouses, beaches, and other facilities. Long- and short-term visitors soon were spending lazy days exploring the wooded hills, the sandy beaches, and the marshes. In spring and summer, fishermen populated the Susquehanna Flats in their search of rockfish, and in fall they pursued tidal bass in the four rivers around the park. Yachtsmen came to try their skills at summer regattas of the North East River Yacht Club. Today the park occupies much of the peninsula between the Northeast and Elk Rivers.

John Smith's quest in 1608 for the Northwest Passage may not have borne fruit for him, but generations since that time have continued to benefit from the natural beauty he discovered during his expeditions in the upper Bay.

There are only a few visitors to the McDaniel Yacht Basin (68) on a postcard-perfect day in 1941. Established in 1929, this famous boatyard survives today as a busy pleasure boat dealer. At nearby Hances Point (69), several spiffy boats await their owners, also in 1941.

White Crystal Beach

In the 1940s teenagers in southern Cecil County thought White Crystal Beach ranked as *the* beach to visit, according to longtime resident Harvey Bossler. Located on the shores of the Elk River near the Chesapeake Bay, the privately run resort had plenty to offer families who vacationed there. Some came to spend the day at the beach where fishermen once dried their nets. Others rented one of the cottages built along the water's edge. Amusements included an arcade with pinball machines and a small duckpin bowling alley. The small boardwalk had other games, such as darts and the ever-popular pitch penny. Two brothers, sons of the original owner, continue to oversee the beach resort today.

On the adjacent property, separated by a fence, Dr. Dorsey L. Lewis and William E. Schultz opened Crystal Beach Manor. Situated on what had been Old Reybold's Wharf Farm, where steamboats once stopped for wheat, tomatoes, and other produce, the 273-acre resort featured a long sandy beach with a view of Turkey Point on the opposite shore. Original construction included 100 cottages, begun in 1934, with an additional 100 lots that awaited future growth. The grounds featured a beautiful shaded picnic ground complete with tables, a bathhouse with showers, and twenty acres for parking. Families from as far away as New Jersey arrived on hot summer days with picnic lunches, ready for a relaxing swim and fun on the beach. Others stayed in the cottages for a lengthier vacation. The old manor house of the farm, shaded by ancient elm trees, provided meals in its elegant dining room and overnight accommodations for weekend guests. Still a thriving private resort, Crystal Beach Manor continues to welcome visitors to its shores.

BEACH PARTIES, WHITE CRYSTAL BEACH, EARLEVILLE, MD.

71

ON THE SANDS, WHITE CRYSTAL BEACH, EARLEVILLE, MD.

THE NIGHTLY DANCE, WHITE CRYSTAL BEACH, EARLEVILLE, MD.

Just up the Elk River from Bay waters, groups of young vacationers seek the sun's warmth (70), while others opt for shade on a summer's day. Some still in street clothes watch from the covered food pavilion (71). As shadows lengthen, the dancing begins (72), later to be crudely lighted by the single strand of naked bulbs. A lone guest contemplates the water from an outdoor deck (73) on what appears to be a wet and cloudy day. Brighter weather brings out cottage renters (74). All of these cards survive from about 1940.

OVERLOOKING THE BAY, WHITE CRYSTAL BEACH, EARLEVILLE, MD.

COTTAGERS ENJOYING THE BEACH, WHITE CRYSTAL BEACH, EARLEVILLE, MD.

Crystal Beach Manor

Anticipating the California surfing craze, boys show off their
"body boards" in this generic linen card from around 1950, advertising
a popular Cecil County beach.

Holloway Beach

I see your back at Holloway Beach, Md.

*Woolen suits in the style of the early 1930s and a clever play on
words highlight this sepia real photo card sent from nearby Charlestown,
Maryland, in August of 1935.*

76

Steamer Susquehanna landing at Betterton, Md.

Betterton

In 1851 Quaker businessman Richard Turner and his wife Elizabeth moved their lumber business from Baltimore to Crew's Landing at the mouth of the Sassafras River on the eastern shore of the Chesapeake Bay. A few years later, after building a house for his family, Turner completed the wharf and renamed the town Betterton, his wife's maiden name. After the Civil War, Richard Turner moved his lumber mill to another location and gave his wife the mill's former property to do with as she pleased.

By this time many sport fishermen had found the small fishing village an excellent place to vacation, but they wished to bring their families along. Elizabeth began dreaming of an amusement pier that everyone could enjoy. Answering the increased demand for board and lodging, James B. Crew built the Chesapeake Hotel (torn down in 1980) and the Owens family built the grocery store, then the Betterton Hotel (destroyed by fire in 1972). Local families took in boarders, fed them good country meals, and charged them a modest $10 to $18 per week. Elizabeth's wish was not realized until 1887 when her husband built the 700-foot amusement pier. Soon after, he built the Rigby Hotel, which raised the level of decorum in town when it demanded that people dress up for dinner.

At the height of Betterton's popularity (1900–1914), seven steamers a day stopped to deposit vacationers for a day, a week, a month, or

Day-trippers fill the pier to start their journey home (77) in this view from the picnic grounds above the beach, postmarked from Betterton on August 13, 1910. A joyful crowd tests the water in front of the wooden amusement center (78) just before World War I. Although this card of straw-hatted men in suits (79) bears a 1939 postmark, the view is probably from a few years earlier.

the whole season. The Ericsson Line, whose vessels continued north to Philadelphia through the C&D Canal, promoted the virtues of a vacation at Betterton, urging potential customers to take advantage of the purity of the air and the pleasant and restful surroundings. "Disciples of Izaak Walton have assured us that at Betterton they have hooked hundreds of fine fish in an hour," their brochure stated, further explaining that passengers on their boats were "in first-class boating trim" when they arrived at Betterton.

At South Broadway in Baltimore family groups loaded down with folding chairs, card tables, and hampers climbed the gangplank of the Wilson Line's steamer, the *Bay Belle,* ready for a day away from the hot summer temperatures of the city. Once aboard they settled into big green easy chairs, or headed to the top deck for a tan, or took to the dance floor. As the *Bay Belle* cruised toward open Bay waters, mothers broke out lunches of cold chicken, homemade crabcakes, and delicious pastries. When the steamer docked at Betterton, runners from the hotels greeted the guests, describing the meals being served that day to those who had arrived without picnic hampers.

After a long, lazy day on what many considered the best bathing beach on the upper Eastern Shore, or hours of fun in the bowling alleys and dance pavilion, sun-soaked families gathered up their belongings and boarded the steamer, ready for an evening of dancing under starlight on the return trip across the Bay. Such excursions continued until 1962. Betterton still serves the area residents, as one of two public beaches in Kent County.

Sassafras Ave., Betterton, Md.

BUSINESS SECTION. BETTERTON. MD.

1—The Pier and Amusement Center, Betterton, Md. on the Chesapeake Bay

6B-H2056

The general store, old-fashioned clear-glass gas pump, and automobiles from the 1920s (80) make this card highly prized by collectors. In a slightly earlier view (81), ladies in long skirts employ their parasols, and few cars line the dusty street. The town appears modern and prosperous and the Bay is an unbelievable shade of blue (82) in this clear linen card from 1936. The same road and sign identify the Hotel Betterton in another 1936 postcard (83). Moved from its original location up the hill, the town's oldest hotel advertised that it was "On the Beach" on the back of this 1950 card (84).

4—Hotel Betterton, Betterton, Md. on the Chesapeake Bay

6B-H2059

9—Hotel Chesapeake and Cottages, Betterton, Maryland

83   84

NEW ARCH ENTRANCE, TOLCHESTER BEACH, MD.

86

The Beach. Tolchester, Md.

Tolchester

*"Bring your lunch and forget your troubles,
out on the deep blue sea.
Wonderful tonic and salt air for the babies."*

Successive generations of city residents responded to this appeal from the Tolchester Steamboat Company to climb aboard one of their steamers for the two-hour, twenty-three-mile trip across the Bay to the cool green splendor of Tolchester Beach. Beginning in 1878 as a crude picnic ground with a few amusements, Tolchester Beach grew over the years to rank as one of the most popular resorts anywhere on the Bay.

Its humble beginnings date to 1877 when Calvin Taggart and his son, E. G. Taggart, operators of a steamship line in Philadelphia, joined with Capt. William C. Eliason to purchase ten acres of land at Tolchester Beach in Kent County. The original idea to connect their steamship line with a railroad being built across the county ended with the bankruptcy of the railroad. In order to utilize the company's steamers and docking facilities at Tolchester and Baltimore, they turned the ten-acre parcel into a primitive amusement park. Over the years Tolchester Beach grew to cover 155 acres, and saw as many as six steamers a day arrive filled with passengers.

The early resort, located on a picturesque tree-crowned bluff, had picnic tables, a bathhouse, a modest hand-cranked merry-go-round, and a

Under the welcoming wooden arches that rose in 1909 (85), the gatekeeper enjoys a calm moment before the next steamer docks on a day in 1920. The backs of the arches and the worn, crude boardwalk are revealed in this card (86), postmarked in 1910. As she did for more than 40 years, the popular Louise (87) disgorges her passengers at the end of the pier in this scene from 1915.

Steamer Louise Landing Excursionists, Tolchester Beach, Md.

88

89

Whirl-Pool Dips, Tolchester Beach, Md.

42

hand organ. Captain Eliason, sympathetic to the temperance movement, immediately set the tone by prohibiting the sale of liquor on the company's steamers. Although skeptics predicted doom from such a stand, other lines quickly followed suit.

In 1881 the company built a beautiful fifty-three-room hotel on top of the bluff. Overnight guests and day-trippers alike sat down to delicious meals in its dining room, where they were served with the grace and style of Eastern Shore tradition. Other visitors preferred to bring along hampers filled with food prepared at home. When the steamer docked, the fastest person from each group of picnickers dashed up the bluff to stake a claim on one of the picnic tables, while the rest of the family followed at a slower pace, carefully transporting the day's food supply. Many wanted to settle near the attractions, the most popular of which was Little Jumbo, a miniature coal-fired steam locomotive built in 1906 at the Baldwin Locomotive Works in Baltimore. With a top speed of eight miles per hour, Little Jumbo, engineered for twenty-five years by Leonard War, used a quarter-ton of coal each day making the two-minute, quarter-mile trips through shaded glades and a tunnel.

In 1922 the humble original merry-go-round gave way to a magnificent model, built originally in 1911 by the Hershell Spillman Company of New York. Children eagerly climbed aboard wild boars, plumed ostriches, a giraffe, a llama, roosters, cats, a stork, leaping frogs, seahorses, and a tiger. They then refreshed themselves with ice cream, made at the resort each day.

Other amusements included a dance hall, the Whirl-Pool Dips roller coaster, baseball dia-

Miniature Train and Excursion Grounds, Tolchester Beach, Md.

TB-5—Miniature Railway and Pennyland, Tolchester Beach, Md., on Chesapeake Bay

5B-H1095

mond, bowling alley, and bridle paths. Many guests chose to sit quietly in the hand-carved chairs on the balcony of the 1909 pavilion, built in the style of an Italian Renaissance villa, and watch the ocean-bound ships glide by on their way to the C&D Canal. Beauty surrounded them in every direction, from the low wrought-iron fence to the rows of peonies, and from the wisteria at the hotel entrance to the fountains sending their cool watery spray high into the air. Tolchester Beach boasted Maryland's first race-track, providing thrills to those visitors interested in harness racing until it closed in 1914. That year also saw the end of the Tolchester Fair, held at the park since the 1890s.

Joseph Goldstein, brother of longtime state comptroller Louis Goldstein, bought the Wilson Steamship Company and Tolchester Beach in 1961. His noble intentions to restore the park to its previous splendor and popularity ended in bankruptcy. In 1962 the steamer *Bay Belle* ceased her summer runs to the park, bringing to a close eighty-five years of Victorian-style splendor on the banks of the Chesapeake Bay.

For most holiday-makers, lunch in the shade (88) was first on the list of activities, as this highly valued 1910 card shows. After allowing a proper interval for digestion, both children and adults headed for the rides, the largest of which was the wooden Whirl-Pool Dips (89). Every seat but one is filled on the Little Jumbo train (90) as it passes the shaded picnic grounds about 1910. Thirty-five years later, the same train pulls out of the amusement area, filled to capacity (91).

The Second Tolchester

92

STEAMER TOLCHESTER, BALTIMORE'S LARGEST EXCURSION STEAMER ON THE WAY TO TOLCHESTER BEACH, MD.

*This iron-hulled side-wheeler became the second Tolchester after many
years of service in New York, Florida, and Virginia. Built in 1878,
she was purchased by the line and brought to Baltimore in 1933, a year
before the date of this early linen card. For eight seasons, she made
two trips daily across the Bay and hosted moonlight cruises in the
evenings; but after burning in her Light Street berth in May of 1941,
she did not sail again as an excursion vessel.*

The Last Tolchester

TB-8—Steamer Tolchester, Baltimore, Md.

8B-H1487

*The third and last boat of its name, and the most modern, this
Tolchester came to Baltimore in 1948, the year this linen card appeared.
With four decks, mostly glass enclosed, it held 2,400 passengers.
By 1950 it remained the only vessel of the Tolchester Company,
and after the 1955 season, was retired to reserve status. Here she
flies the line's red and blue flag as vacationers crowd the
bow and enjoy the view from the top deck.*

Rock Hall

Nestled near Swan Point at the mouth of the Chester River in Kent County, the village of Rock Hall dates to 1707 when Capt. Thomas Harris purchased the waterfront land and operated two grain boats, the *Levant* and the *Thomas Harris*. Although the packet ferries from Annapolis delivered mail, passengers, and products to Bowly's Wharf three times a week, wharf-owner Harris resisted the accommodation of steamboats for a time, forcing them to land two miles away at Gray's Inn.

In 1781 Lt. Col. Tench Tilghman, aide-de-camp to George Washington, rode the Annapolis packet ferry to Rock Hall, the ferry's northern terminus and the post road's southern terminus, on his way from Yorktown to Philadelphia to tell the Continental Congress of Lord Cornwallis's surrender.

Fishing, the main business of Rock Hall, enticed sportsmen young and old to visit the serene blue waters of the Bay to try their luck at landing the elusive quarry that included rockfish, white perch, herring, and shad. While hunters regarded Swan Point as one of the finest spots for bagging wild fowl, watermen knew the area for its excellent oysters and clams.

Year-round residents enjoyed the clear bracing air in winter and the excellent sea bathing in summer. Vacationers soon discovered the benefits of the simple life at Rock Hall, where time slowed to a more healthful pace, and they began taking advantage of the water activities and leisurely lifestyle.

Early visitors from Baltimore stepped aboard one of the vessels of the Chester River Steamboat Company at Pier 7 Light Street for the hour-and-

STEAMER B. S. FORD, APPROACHING PIER, ROCK HALL, MD.

17—View of Harbor and Jettie overlooking the Chesapeake Bay, Rock Hall, Md.

5B-H1108

18—Main Street Looking South, Rock Hall, Md.

5B-H1109

16—Harbor and Marine Railway, Rock Hall, Md.

5B-H1107

forty-minute run across the Bay. In 1919 the Baltimore and Eastern Shore Ferry Line began service from Bay Shore to Rock Hall.

In the heat of a 1920s summer, visitors and residents sat down at the cool marble counter of Durding's Store on Main Street, opened originally by a member of the Merck family, and sipped a cool drink or ate a luscious dessert prepared at the gleaming chrome soda fountain, a treat that continues today.

In 1938 the formation of the Rock Hall Yacht Club brought the first regatta to area waters. In August of that same year Rock Hall hosted the Fishing Fair, which became an annual event put on by the Chesapeake Bay Fishing Fair Association. The Pennsylvania Railroad even ran "fishing trains" to Chestertown and provided buses to carry visitors the final thirteen miles to the port.

Water activities remain in the heart and soul of Rock Hall, where seafood packing houses have been replaced with marinas and pleasure craft of every description line the numerous floating docks.

In a card highly prized by collectors of Bay scenes for its detail and its 1923 Rock Hall postmark (94), one of the Bay's largest steamers is about to tie up. She was built by the Chester River Steamboat Company in 1877. By contrast with the earlier busyness, in this 1945 view the harbor (95) seems deserted but brightened by trim wooden boats, and an imaginative sunset. Main Street (96) displays small-town charm and orderliness, as well as a victory flag, in the same year. Also in 1945, the marina and harbor (97) make but a small part of the waterfront when viewed from the Bay.

B. C. & A. Wharf, Claiborne, Md.

Claiborne, Md.

Claiborne

Situated on a point of land jutting out into Eastern Bay, east of the southern tip of Kent Island, the village of Claiborne began in 1631 as a fort that served as a base for an Indian and fur-trading post, and was named for its founder, Virginia colonist William Claiborne. Three years later Leonard Calvert, the younger son of Lord Baltimore, sailed up the Bay with the *Ark* and the *Dove* and discovered Claiborne's fort within the boundaries of his father's 1632 grant. He considered Claiborne a trespasser and made plans to drive him from the area. Claiborne hung on as long as possible but finally fled in 1635.

In 1894 the Baltimore, Chesapeake and Atlantic Railroad (also affectionately known as the Black Cinders and Ashes) ran the excursion steamer *Cambridge* between Baltimore and Claiborne. Leaving Pier 8 at Light Street, the *Cambridge* carried her excursion passengers on a steadfast course toward Eastern Bay. As on other such trips, her passengers came prepared with lunch baskets or boxes filled with Maryland fried chicken, vine-ripened tomatoes, juicy peaches, and more. Others enjoyed a delicious lunch of country ham in the steamer's dining room. Two trains waited at Claiborne, one the express *Ocean City Flyer,* the other a local that made numerous stops before finally reaching Ocean City. This rail-steamboat service provided a vital link between eastern and western shores for passengers and freight, but it handled no automobiles.

With the announcement of a Claiborne-Annapolis ferry service, that situation changed. The steamer *Governor Emerson C. Harrington,* a side-wheeler whose center was hollowed out to accommodate up to thirty-five cars, began service in 1919.

REGATTA AT CLAIBOURNE, NEAR EASTON, MD.

HAND-COLORED

CLAIBORNE—ANNAPOLIS FERRY.

JOHN M. DENNIS.

Brave and daring passengers drove their own cars onto the steamer at King George Street in Annapolis. In the mid-1920s she was joined by a double-ended ferry, the *Albert C. Ritchie,* and in 1929 by the diesel-powered *John M. Dennis,* a large ferry capable of carrying 100 cars. Her interior, featuring four winding staircases and mahogany paneling, reflected the colonial architecture of Annapolis.

Not everyone merely passed through Claiborne, on the way to other points. From 1925 to 1944 children whose parents suffered from tuberculosis traveled to Claiborne each summer for a ten-week vacation at Miracle House, founded by William B. Matthews, Sr., the managing director of the Maryland Tuberculosis Association. When new treatments for preventing the spread of the parents' disease were developed the home was closed.

Claiborne remained the "front door to the Eastern Shore" until the mid-1930s, when the shorter route from Sandy Point to Matapeake, which ferries began using in 1930, permanently replaced the longer Annapolis-Claiborne journey. Instead, travelers on their way to Ocean City drove their vehicles from Matapeake down Kent Island to Romancoke to take the shuttle ferry over to Claiborne. Matapeake service continued until July 1952 when the Chesapeake Bay Bridge opened.

Two locomotives, a steamship at the landing, and the fact that it was issued by the nearby McDaniel publisher make this card (98) from about 1910 unusually desirable. In a longer view (99), postmarked from St. Michaels in the following year, the sender notes "This is where we take the boat to Baltimore." The waters off Claiborne provide an ideally calm setting for an annual regatta (100), in this elegant and softly hand-colored view from 1909. Replaced in 1952 by the brand new Bay Bridge, the John M. Dennis (101) ferried cars and passengers from Annapolis, and later Sandy Point, around the southern end of Kent Island to Claiborne for many years. In this bright card from the 1930s, she carries yet another load to the Eastern Shore.

St. Michaels

Hailed by many as the "Pearl of the Chesapeake Bay," St. Michaels lies on a neck of land between the Miles River and Broad Creek, southeast of Claiborne. The combination of waterfront on one side and miles of lush forests on the other makes St. Michaels one of the most picturesque ports in Maryland.

Verrazano first explored the peninsula in 1524, followed by John Smith in 1608. William Claiborne referred to the area as Shipping Creek in 1633 because of its high level of activity as a trading center. Early in its history colonists declared St. Michaels a free port in order to attract rich cargoes that were free of duty charges. The name of town and river dates to 1677 and the formation of the Episcopal parish, named for St. Michael the Archangel. With the influx of Quakers to the area and their dislike for saintly titles, the river became Michaels, then eventually Miles.

The town's deepwater harbor attracted ship-builders and sailors, and by 1812 St. Michaels was producing large numbers of clipper ships and sailing produce carriers. The corner of Carpenter and Locust Streets, home to numerous taverns, soon acquired the name Hell's Crossing, because of the street fights that broke out there between feisty sailors after a night on the town. A ship's carpenter's bell, cast in 1842, tolled four times a day, telling the boatbuilders when to begin work, to start and stop their midday meal, and to quit for the day. In the early 1890s the bell was retired from service and given to the town.

Fishermen, hunters, and people looking for relaxation in the midst of natural beauty came to St. Michaels in large numbers. The Bay side of

Scene near St. Michaels, Md.

no. 6256

103

"DREAMLAND," ST. MICHAELS, MD.

COPYRIGHT 1908, BY THOS. H. SEWELL

1551 The Bridge, St. Michaels, Md.

town offered scores of coves and myriad tiny inlets where shellfish flourished. The well-protected banks provided shelter for large numbers of shore birds. Excursion steamers filled with day-trippers shoved off from Baltimore early in the morning for the four-hour cruise to Navy Point. Upon docking, hundreds of picnickers disembarked ready for a day of food and fun. One resident, R. S. Dodson, recalled in a 1965 *Evening Sun* article that most visitors were peaceful and pleasant, but some tried to picnic on residents' lawns, or made themselves at home on people's porches, or even raided private fruit trees. Youngsters in town made extra spending money by setting up lemonade and watermelon stands. Mr. Dodson, then a boy of five, charged other children 2 cents each for rides around Navy Point on his burro, Maria.

An increased interest in log canoe racing on the Miles River led members of the St. Michaels poker club to organize the Miles River Yacht Club in the summer of 1920 with the further purpose of developing sail, yacht, and motorboat racing on the Chesapeake Bay. In 1927 the club began awarding the Governor's Cup trophy to each year's winner of the club's log canoe race. The yachtsmen's spirits were not dampened even by the Great Depression, during which as many as a thousand boats appeared for the summer regattas.

Log canoes race on the Bay in this sunny card (102) post-marked from St. Michaels on July 18, 1912. Grand old willows shade a path along the waterfront (103) on a summer day in this card from 1909. A typical tidewater estate (104) sits right on the shore in this card sent from Claiborne to Baltimore in the same year. On a Saturday or Sunday afternoon in 1908, when cards such as this (105) were two for a nickel in every souvenir shop and corner store, a crowd fills the wooden bridge, probably to watch a sailboat race.

THE MAGIC, CHESAPEAKE BAY LOG CANOE CHAMPION, ST. MICHAELS, MD.

106

Tilghman Island fishing grounds and the Eastern Shore inland waterway, or swam at the Oakwood Inn's protected bathing beaches. The Wades Point Inn, located on a point of land overlooking the Bay, began welcoming guests in 1899. Thomas Kemp built the main house of the inn in 1819, seven years after building the clipper schooner, *Chasseur,* the original "Pride of Baltimore," at a

WATERFRONT, OAKWOOD INN, ST. MICHAELS, MARYLAND

107

Racing enthusiasts from all over the Bay arrived each summer to compete, many staying at the Chelsea Hotel, the unofficial headquarters for regatta visitors and yachtsmen until fire destroyed it in late 1941. Hardier, more adventuresome water-race followers pitched tents along the shore or slept in their boats or even on the yacht club lawn.

Other vacationers stayed at the Oakwood Inn located on the waterfront. When not participating in racing, they took boat tours through the

Fells Point boatyard. Other people stayed at the Inn at Perry Cabin, built in 1820 by Samuel Hambleton and named as a tribute to Commodore Oliver Hazard Perry, under whom he had served. The Inn at Perry Cabin continues to welcome guests to the banks of the Miles River.

MAIN STREET, ST. MICHAELS, MD.

109

BENEATH THE SHOWERS, OAKWOOD INN, ST. MICHAELS, MD.

108

A larger and more complex descendant of hand-hewn Native American boats, the Chesapeake Bay log canoe has been a popular sailing craft since the seventeenth century. Originally constructed with a single dugout log bottom, and later by joining two logs to form a keel, these boats remain graceful and timeless. Here, the crew of the famous Magic (106) guides the boat in a 1950s race.

Actually on the little Santo Domingo River, the Oakwood Inn boasted in a 1953 flyer that it sat "right on the waterfront, removed from highway and traffic dangers." The pavilion stands almost deserted while a lone sailboat docks (107). Swimmers enjoy a quick wash-off (108) as they leave the pier, likely anticipating the inn's famous country-style all-you-can-eat dinners for $2.25. Black-and-white views such as these survived until about 1960, as did this sleepy image of St. Michaels (109), postmarked from there on September 21, 1959, looking down what was at other times named Talbot Street and Front Street.

THE PASADENA — ROYAL OAK, MARYLAND

AIR VIEW OF BEAUTIFUL PASADENA INN — ROYAL OAK, MARYLAND 1B-H1107

The Pasadena Inn

At the turn of the twentieth century, summer visitors to Royal Oak, near St. Michaels in Talbot County, had few choices for overnight accommodations. Then the need for extra income for farm expenses prompted Frederick and Louise Harper to follow the lead of other area residents and open their home to guests. Beginning in 1902 the Harpers advertised in the Baltimore and Washington newspapers for summer boarders at a reasonable price. Soon guests arrived in welcome numbers, traveling by steamer from the Western Shore to Claiborne, then by train to Royal Oak. The community reportedly took its name from a British attack on St. Michaels in 1812, when a cannonball lodged in a giant oak tree.

The Harpers bought their place in 1884. The house had been built in 1784, and the farm, known as Oak Hall, was originally part of a 1680 land grant to the Benson family by Lord Baltimore. The house-turned-hotel took its name from the town of Pasadena, California, because Harper relatives had written enthusiastic reports of their visits there. In 1929 Gary Cooper and Faye Wray stayed at the inn during the filming of the silent movie, "The First Kiss," in Easton. Ms. Wray's wedding took place aboard a skipjack in the Chesapeake Bay.

The Harper family continued operating the inn until 1971, when they sold the property to Schwaben International, a German company, which ran it as a company resort and conference center. In 1996 new owners purchased the property and, after extensive renovations, reopened it as The Oaks, a country inn.

Still exuding a genteel air, the original eighteenth-century house welcomes guests at the end of a tree-lined drive (110) in this card from about 1960. An "air view" from twenty years earlier (111) reveals the extent of the Pasadena Inn's holdings and includes five tiny boats, all added by the artist.

Easton

THE ANCHORAGE - MILES RIVER,
...TON, MD.

MUSIC HALL, PLAZA AND COURT HOUSE, EASTON, MD.

113

The town of Easton, county seat of Talbot County and long considered the colonial capital of the Eastern Shore, sits on fertile land near the headwaters of the Tred Avon River. Originally called Talbot Courthouse, Easton dates to around 1661, when the area that became the town served as the administrative center of Talbot County. Named for Grace Talbot, sister of Cecilius Calvert and daughter of Lord Baltimore, Talbot County ranks as the second oldest county on the Eastern Shore. The first courthouse, erected in 1710 at a cost of 115,000 pounds of tobacco, housed its first hearings in 1712. People attending court stayed at a nearby tavern or "ordinary" run by Elizabeth Winkles, a landlord who reportedly "knew how to keep a hotel." In March 1785 an act authorizing the building of the town passed. The name changed in 1788 to Easton, derived from East Town, the popular name for Talbot Courthouse. A second courthouse replaced the original 20' x 30' structure in 1794.

Life continued quietly in the mainly agricultural county, residents preferring to remain off the beaten path of progress. Easton's first hotel, the Brick, did not appear until 1812; train service arrived in 1869. Even though the nearest landing was a mile away at Easton Point on the Tred Avon River, the town's residents led active lives on the water, fishing, crabbing, duckhunting, or sailing. Because of Easton's location on the route to Ocean City and the towns of the lower Eastern Shore, as well as Philadelphia and Delaware, more

One of Talbot County's and Maryland's most noted colonial estates, the Anchorage (112) rests on the banks of the Miles River in this hand-colored card from before World War I. Here (113), the center of Easton is visited by a handsome team of horses and a stylish automobile with its top down on a day in the 1920s. Few towns in America can boast a plaza that includes a 1794 courthouse.

55

people discovered the quiet little town that tried to keep itself free from the turmoil of the modern world. A need to accommodate the growing number of visitors, however, led to the formation in 1889 of a company for the purpose of building and operating a new hostelry. In 1891 the Avon Hotel opened and quickly gained the reputation for being one of the best in the area. The smaller Hotel Queen Anne followed in 1918. When fire destroyed the Avon in 1944, the Queen Anne became Easton's only hotel, the Brick having closed some years earlier.

In 1885 while sitting off Oxford on the deck of William O'Sullivan Dimpfel's yacht, *Gaetina,* area yachtsmen formed the Chesapeake Bay Yacht Club, one of the oldest yacht clubs in the country. Avid sailing enthusiasts arrived in increasing numbers each summer to race in the Chesapeake Bay Yacht Club's regattas, competing for various trophies. Sir Thomas Lipton presented the trophy to the winner in the Star Class in 1926. Mr. and Mrs. Eliot Wheeler gave the Commodore's Club trophy, first presented in 1932 to the winning Chesapeake Bay log canoe, as a memorial to past commodores.

One yachtsman, A. Johnson Grymes, who owned an estate on Bailey's Neck, did more than compete. Hailing from a family prominent in New Jersey shipbuilding circles, Mr. Grymes engaged New York architect, Frank A. Bower, to design a hotel that reflected the colonial character of Easton's best homes and public buildings. On September 3, 1949, after three years of careful thought and planning, the Tidewater Inn opened its doors on the site of the Avon Hotel. Since that

114

Ratcliffe Manor, near Easton, Md.

115

HOTEL AVON, EASTON, MD.

"WHERE GRACIOUS PLENTY RULES THE BOARD"

QUEEN ANNE HOTEL, EASTON, MD.

HOPE HOUSE, EASTON, MD.

7A359

time, generations of visitors have stopped to enjoy an elegant lunch of panned rockfish or soft-shell crabs on their way to Ocean City, while others have chosen to stay for several days, preferring to swim at the inn's private beach and to take advantage of Easton's fishing, duckhunting, and sailing.

Ratcliffe Manor (114) sits proudly, even if almost totally engulfed in ivy, on its original 300-acre land grant in this circa-1915 hand-colored card. Is that the family dog the photographer has captured in the lower right-hand corner? A charming wooden structure, the Avon Hotel (115) stood at the corner of Dover and Harris Streets from 1891 until it burned down in a spectacular fire in January of 1944. Guests take advantage of the shady porch in this view from about 1925. Guests and friends (116) enjoy the comfortable rockers and immaculate grounds at the smaller Queen Anne Hotel, also circa 1925. By the time this postcard of Hope House (117) appeared in 1937, the grounds had been transformed into a 500-acre arboretum by its owner, Mrs. Ida M. Starr. With over 150 species, it included every kind of tree grown in Maryland. Mrs. Starr, who died in 1938, recalled that when she and her husband bought the house, it was nothing but "a staircase and a view." They completely restored the historic residence from plans found in the attic.

B. C. & A. Steamboat Wharf.   Oxford, Maryland.

118

OXFORD REGATTA, YACHTS ASSEMBLED AT "RADCLIFFE," AUG. 1909.

Yachts at Anchor.   Oxford, Maryland.

Oxford

Even before its official founding as a town and port in 1683, Oxford owed its history to the water. Because of its strategic location on a peninsula of land bounded by the Choptank and Tred Avon Rivers and Town Creek, the settlement attracted sea captains, eager to trade their cargoes. Eleven years later the colony's legislators named Oxford, one of Talbot County's oldest towns, the only official port of entry on the Eastern Shore and instructed commissioners to survey the land and divide it into lots. Oxford's shipping economy boomed, inspiring boatbuilders to settle there and construct some of the finest ships on the seas. By the 1730s ships from Britain to Spain to Africa called at the port with their cargoes of molasses, rum, oranges, wine, and slaves to exchange for Maryland's fine tobacco, wood products, grain, livestock, bricks, and animal hides.

Robert Morris, a name intimately connected with Oxford, arrived from Liverpool in 1738 as representative for the English mercantile company, Foster Cunliffe & Sons. Until his untimely death in 1750, Morris actively participated in the port's many activities. His son, Robert Morris, Jr., who joined him in 1748, went on to become financier of the American Revolution.

Referred to as Thread Haven, Third Haven, or Tred Avon at various times, Oxford became Williamstadt in 1695, but reverted to Oxford in 1702 when Queen Anne ascended the throne in

A steamer, probably the Talbot from Annapolis, glides into its temporary berth at the Town Point Wharf (118) in this early hand-colored card. Sailboats of several classes await the start of the August Regatta (119), an Oxford tradition, in this hand-colored card from 1909. A log canoe and a dinghy slip by yachts at anchor (120) under an unnaturally pink sky in about the same year.

England following the death of King William. Although no one seems to be certain, Thread Haven may date from the days when linen and cordage were shipped from the port.

With the growth of Baltimore and Annapolis to the north and the end of trade with Britain during the American Revolution, Oxford fell from favor as a port and slipped from the limelight of the mercantile world.

The post–Civil War years brought renewed prosperity to Oxford, as boatbuilders there developed cargo schooners, bugeyes (an enlarged version of the log canoe), and skipjacks. In 1871 the Maryland and Delaware Railroad finally completed its line into Oxford, further expanding trade in the area. Steamboats bringing passengers and freight from Baltimore and Annapolis docked at the wharves on Town Point.

Summer day-trippers climbed aboard the Baltimore steamers *Joppa, Avalon,* and *Chesapeake* for the journey down the Bay. Other visitors arrived by train or over rough oyster-shell roads to enjoy the sea air and summer activities. Vacationers stayed at area hotels including the Eastford Hall Hotel (destroyed by fire in 1894), the Riverview Hotel (later renamed the Robert Morris Inn), Sinclair House, and Grapevine House. Large rooming houses and individual homes also took in boarders. Besides fishing, crabbing, and sailing, families could attend theatrical productions and movies at the Red Men's Hall, built in 1910, or free summer concerts in Town Park.

121

Public Square, Oxford, Maryland.

122

TRED AVON YACHT CLUB, OXFORD, MD.

Morris Street   Oxford, Maryland

Sixty years before the founding of the Tred Avon Yacht Club in 1931, working watermen held impromptu competitions while returning to port. In 1927 Oxford hosted the Seventh Annual Chesapeake Bay Championship Workboat Regatta, conceived by the *Sunpapers* of Baltimore. The competition brought schooners, bugeyes, skipjacks, workboats, and skiffs to area waters. Log canoes raced in the Yacht Club's annual regattas and began competing for the Capt. Buck Richardson Trophy in 1957.

Today's residents and visitors alike continue to ride the Tred Avon Ferry, which carries passengers between Oxford and Bellevue as it has done in one form or another since it began service in 1683 as a scow. The water continues to be the main draw in Oxford, attracting pleasure boats to its waters as it has done for hundreds of years.

124

TWO RECENTLY FINISHED BUILDINGS IN OXFORD, MD.

With the Tred Avon in the background, the Public Square of Oxford (121) provides shade and a wide lawn for relaxing in this card postmarked from Oxford on July 16, 1912. Almost thirty years later, in the middle of World War II, the modest new home of the Tred Avon Yacht Club (122) sits quietly at Town Point. The perfect photo of a 1920s filling station (123) makes this view of Oxford's main street highly prized. One of the new buildings in this 1940s card of the town's waterfront (124) appears to be a public toilet.

Cambridge

Probably named for the English university town, Cambridge dates to 1684, when Col. John Kirk, a Scottish promoter, came across the Choptank River from Talbot County and bought 100 acres of land. Three years later, when the Dorchester County court met there, Cambridge became the county seat.

Because of its sheltered location on the Choptank River some fifteen miles from the Chesapeake Bay and its abundance of forest filled with white oak, Cambridge became a center of shipbuilding early in the eighteenth century. Coastal and ocean-going vessels regularly sailed in from all over the world. The flat, fertile land yielded excellent tobacco crops; the waters provided oysters, crabs, fish, and terrapin; while the marshes brought forth muskrats and ducks. For a time, huge oyster-shucking plants flourished on Long Wharf, their production rivaling that of Norfolk to the south. In the early twentieth century, when oyster packing leveled off, businesses turned to canning tomatoes instead.

Mornings when the steamboats from Baltimore docked at Long Wharf brought great excitement to the sleepy town. In the late nine-

What appears to be the calm of early morning on the Choptank is enlivened by the shrimp-hued sky in this lovely card (125) postmarked from Cambridge on April 13, 1926. The famous Talbot (126), described on the back of this card as one of the line's "palatial night steamers," rests at the end of her long nocturnal run from Baltimore on a clear morning in about the same year. Earlier in that same decade, a mostly male crowd have parked their snappy autos and gathered along the wharf to watch the weekend sailboat races (127), a popular summer tradition sponsored by the local yacht club.

THE HARBOR FROM STEAMSHIP PIER, CAMBRIDGE, MD.

125

126

B. C. & A. STEAMER TALBOT AT WHARF, CAMBRIDGE, MD.

Watching the Boat Races at Cambridge, Md.

teenth century no fewer than three different companies ran steamers down the Bay to the Choptank. The Maryland Steamboat Company sent the *Enoch Pratt,* the *Ida,* and the *Joppa.* The *Minnie Wheeler,* a side-wheeler constructed in 1881, sailed for the Wheeler Line. And the *Choptank, Tred Avon,* and *Cambridge* carried passengers and freight for the Choptank Steamboat Company. In 1894 the Baltimore, Chesapeake and Atlantic Railroad Company purchased the three rival firms, and the number of vessels visiting Cambridge declined. Not that the citizens of Cambridge always welcomed the excursion boats. For a time the mayor and town council refused landing permits for Sundays, because they disliked the crude behavior of a number of the day-trippers. Some strolled through the streets drinking liquor from bottles while others blithely walked over residents' lawns. Town fathers displayed a similar reaction during World War II when sailors came across from the naval stations on the Patuxent River. By 1930, after further mergers affected steamboat service, only the *Calvert* operated to the Choptank. The rise in popularity of the automobile no doubt contributed to the failure of the steamboat company in 1932, sharply curtailing passenger steamer service to Cambridge.

Summer visitors congregated at Oakley Beach, named for the famous sharpshooter, Annie Oakley, who with her husband, Frank Butler, retired to Cambridge from 1913 to 1915. During those years, Ms. Oakley often invited neighborhood children or the local Girl Scout troop to her house for shooting demonstrations. When her performance concluded, she served them cool glasses of pink

128

HOTEL DIXON, CAMBRIDGE, MD.

129

7—Oakley Beach Hotel, Cambridge, Md.

HIGH STREET, LOOKING TOWARDS RIVER FROM YACHT CLUB,
CAMBRIDGE, MD.

Yacht Club, Cambridge, Maryland

13

lemonade. The nearby Oakley Hotel, a three-story wooden structure, welcomed summer vacationers and winter duckhunters until it was destroyed by fire in 1954. The Cambridge Hotel, another landmark in town, burned in 1958 after fifty years of catering to the families who vacationed there. In the 1930s cool ice cream sodas awaited patrons of the High Spot Restaurant on High Street and Hyser's Old Time Soda Fountain on Locust Street.

A fortuitous meeting in 1909 between Alfred I. du Pont and W. L. Barrett led to the founding of the Cambridge Yacht Club. Mr. du Pont, aboard his yacht *Alicia,* was sailing off Long Wharf. Mr. Barrett, whose boat used the newest fuel, gasoline, ran circles around the *Alicia,* piquing du Pont's curiosity. As a result of their discussions, du Pont decided to set up the new club, at his own expense. Twenty-nine years later Francis du Pont of Wilmington, Delaware, presented the town with a new clubhouse, on the edge of the Choptank in Municipal Park. Boat racing figured prominently in the annual events of the club, attracting pleasure craft from all over the Bay.

With one of the finest harbors on the Eastern Shore, Cambridge continues to appeal to boaters of all descriptions, and it promotes itself as "a pleasant place to live."

The mansard roof of the Hotel Dixon (128) lends a graceful air to High Street. Parking regulations seem nonexistent in this detailed view from about 1918. Named for famous "sure shot" Annie Oakley, the Oakley Beach Hotel (129) welcomes guests in this 1935 linen card. Further down High Street (130), impressive houses line both sides in this card bearing a 1916 postmark. An army of folding chairs waits in loose formation outside the sporty streamline-style Yacht Club (131).

Waterview

132

Properly dressed hotel guests rub shoulders with watermen and
their families in the hotel dining room, flowers bloom in unusually
bright shades, and locals pose on the pier in this imaginatively colored
multiview linen card from about 1940. At the mouth of the Nanticoke
River and just down Route 349 from Bivalve and Jestertown, tiny
Waterview offers quiet days, good fishing, and spectacular Bay sunsets.

Crisfield

Boat Landing and Railroad Station, Crisfield, Md.

OB-H810

133

Fishing boats lie at anchor and seabirds wait for their dinner at the landing on a perfect afternoon in 1940. Home of the Hard Crab Derby, "Miss Crustacean," and Labor Day races, Crisfield enjoys its reputation as the "Soft Crab Capital of the World" but retains its emblems of oyster and clam shells. Packing houses dumped enormous piles of oyster shells, prompting natives to recall, "They shipped out the oysters and lived on the shells."

People and Postcards

For many collectors, the backs of cards are as important as the fronts. Stamps, cancellations, and postmarks can add value, but the messages vacationers and business travelers sent home allow us to share a moment in their lives.

Racing, Fishing, Boating, Gunning, Indoor Pool, Dancing. Rail, Motor and Boat facilities. Midway between Washington and New York. Garage.

POST CARD

THIS SPACE FOR ADDRESS ONLY.

HAVRE DE GRACE MD. MAY 14 11 A.M. 1928

2 CENTS

BALTIMORE STEAM PACKET CO.
(OLD BAY LINE)

The Oldest Line   The Newest Boats

The Best Service

BETWEEN

BALTIMORE   NORFOLK   OLD POINT
AND PORTSMOUTH, VA.

On Board New Steamer "State of Virginia"

Dearest Grandmother

Post Card

THIS SPACE FOR ADDRESS ONLY

BALT'O. & NORF. 1928

2 CENTS

Mrs. Ida J. Bass

CARD

FORTRESS MONROE, VA. JAN 23 4 PM 1908

This space is for the Address only

Mr. Henry Derby

BEVERLEY BEACH CLUB
On CHESAPEAKE BAY, MD.

Salt water bathing day and night
9 A.M. to 11 P.M.

Dancing every night, 8:15 to 11:45 P.M.
Music by JIMMIE ELLIOTT'S ORCHESTRA

Say - this place is the real thing. Nothing else like it in Maryland. Drive down and get in the swim. I'll be looking for you.

Jack

P.S. Ask the gateman for a free membership card.

Rittenhouse Motor Lodge

U.S. Route #13
Cape Charles, Virginia

7 Miles North of Kiptopeke Ferry — Located on Right for Southbound traffic — Left for North-bound

EXCELLENT APPOINTMENTS

Phone — Cape Charles: 668
or
Write Box 288, Cape Charles, Va.

Mr. & Mrs. Robert M. Rittenhouse — Owner-Mgr.

CAPE CHARLES, VA. FEB 18 1958

POST CARD

2c U.S. POSTAGE

STAYED-IN-N-J-YESTERDAY
PIKE-O-K-TODAY-#13-ALL-ICE
FOR-80-MILES-&-DRIFTING-LIKE-H
AT-TIMES-COULD'NT-SEE-WHERE
I-WAS-GOING. WILL-TAKE-FERRY
ACROSS-CHESAPEAKE-BAY
TOMORROW. WE-ARE-ONLY-12-MILES
AWAY-FROM-IT-TONIGHT. HOPE
YOU-DONT-GET-THAT-STORM
VERY-COLD-HERE-TONIGHT
HOPE-EVERY-THING-O-K-L&F

MISS. LURA HOIT
R.F.D. #2
HAMPDEN-HLD'S
ME.

THIS SPACE FOR WRITING MESSAGES   116695

POST CARD

THIS SPACE FOR ADDRESS ONLY

Miss Lemora Sullivan

POST CARD

BAY
SHORE
SERIES

POST CARD

THIS SIDE FOR CORRESPONDENCE.   THE ADDRESS TO BE WRITTEN ON THIS SIDE

Mr Jacob Morris

POST CARD

Mr + Mrs. Arthur W. Bachman

B. C. & A. STEAMER TALBOT AT
WHARF, CAMBRIDGE, MD.

Cambridge is blessed with excellent railroad and
steamboat facilities. Here is shown one of the popular
night steamers plying between Baltimore and Cambridge.

POST CARD

THIS SPACE FOR ADDRESS ONLY

Mr. Kenneth Johnson

Lewisburg. R. D. 3

Penna.

Mrs Cora Oberholtzer

Bechtelsville

Pa.

Post Cards of Quality—The Albertype Co., Brooklyn, N. Y.

69

BAND CONCERT

HOTEL CHAMBERLIN
GEO. F. ADAMS, MGR.
FORTRESS MONROE, VA.

EAST FRONT

BOAT LANDING, OLD POINT COMFORT, VA.

122882

Old Point Comfort

While exploring the lower Chesapeake Bay in July 1608, Capt. John Smith and his party encountered a ferocious storm. Their open boat exposed them to the full intensity of the blast, and they fought to find their way to a safe harbor. Pushing south past the York River and Back Creek, they finally came to a sandy spit of land jutting out into the mouth of the James River. Upon rounding the point, they found shelter from the storm, and they promptly named the spit Point Comfort. In time the "Old" was added to distinguish it from New Point Comfort up the Bay. Since Smith's time many ships have found safety there, including the French fleet prior to Cornwallis's surrender at Yorktown. In 1862 the *Monitor* and the *Virginia* (formerly the *Merrimac*) met in the waters of Hampton Roads, just beyond Point Comfort, for their inconclusive battle.

As early as the 1830s, Old Point Comfort was best known as a fashionable summer resort where people gathered to enjoy the luxuries of seabathing and fishing or to amuse themselves in the billiard saloons, bowling alleys, or pistol galleries. The outbreak of the Civil War led to the demolition of the Hygeia Hotel and use of the point as an important Union military post. Several years after the conflict, the Hygeia rose again, restoring Old Point Comfort to its position as a premier resort.

Steamers from Baltimore made regular trips down the Chesapeake Bay to Virginia as early as 1840, delivering many vacationers to Old Point Comfort for a relaxing and soothing holiday in the healthful climate. In 1914 the Hotel Chamberlin advertised that it had the finest baths and seapools in America, and medicinal baths complete in every detail. "An ideal resort for rest and

OLD POINT LIGHT, FORTRESS MONROE, VA.

SHERWOOD INN. OLD POINT COMFORT, VA.

recuperation which combines ease of access, equable climate, interesting surroundings, correct sanitation, with perfect hotel accommodations." The nearby Sherwood Inn offered a "pleasant, attractive and comfortable home to those seeking health or pleasure."

In April 1928 the expanded 300-room Chamberlin-Vanderbilt Hotel opened, offering its patrons golf, tennis, indoor saltwater swimming, yachting, fishing, and therapeutic treatments, "all in the atmosphere of Fortress Monroe with its brilliant gathering of officers of the Army, Navy, and Air Forces."

The strategic position of Old Point Comfort had led to the building of a fort there as early as 1630. The Virginia legislature ceded the land to the U.S. Government to be used as a military post, and in 1817 work began on the building of Fortress Monroe, an irregular hexagon covering eighty acres of ground. Old Point Comfort Light, built in 1802, is the oldest standing structure at the fort, and one of the oldest lighthouses of the Chesapeake Bay area. Still operational, the fifty-four-foot octagonal tower with its fourth order Fresnel lens installed in the 1850s, continues to guide vessels to the Hampton Roads harbor.

Just prior to World War I, sailors parade in front of the original Hotel Chamberlin (134). Adjoining the hotel's grounds, the busy boat landing (135) accommodates two steamers, a couple of bright trolleys, and upwards of two dozen autos in this card postmarked in 1936. In a view from about the same year, the Old Point Light (136) and its keeper's house appear freshly cleaned and immaculately trimmed against the spring landscape. The neatly painted Sherwood Inn (137) flaunts its festive awnings in the midday sun, as a carriage and team pause on one side and an extremely early auto sits on another in this sharp photo view postmarked January 23, 1908.

71

Hampton Roads

Steamers traveling on from Old Point Comfort to Norfolk passed through the busy waters of Hampton Roads, the name given to the area where the James, Elizabeth, and Nansemond Rivers flow into the Chesapeake Bay. The convergence of these bodies of water forms the world's finest deep-water harbor and has led to Hampton Roads' involvement in numerous naval occupations and battles since the early seventeenth century. The name Hampton honors Henry Wriothesley, Earl of Southampton and supporter of the colonization of Virginia in the early seventeenth century.

With access to the Atlantic Ocean and the vast Chesapeake Bay, Hampton Roads has long welcomed vessels of every size and description. Ships laden with settlers and their supplies coming to Virginia sailed through Hampton Roads to the James River and up to Yorktown and beyond. Beginning in the midnineteenth century, ships of the Old Bay Line, the Chesapeake Steamship Company, and the Merchants and Miners Line steamed through these waters, delivering their passengers from Baltimore to the individual ports of the area. Often those passengers took delight in seeing the Atlantic fleet anchored here, as well as ocean-going freight and passenger ships.

Hampton Roads' strategic location quickly made it a valuable military asset, attracting bases representing all the branches of America's forces, especially the Navy, as well as the headquarters for NATO and the Armed Forces Staff College. Today seven of the country's largest military installations reside in Hampton Roads.

138

Hampton Roads showing the Harbor and Casino at Newport News, Va.

139

3014—"Hampton Roads", Va., Showing Pine Beach Pier.

140

Two schooners and several smaller wooden vessels ride at anchor amid newer iron-hulled ships (138) on a clear day in about 1910. At least three years earlier, the view in another direction (139) shows the popularity of sailing and of the amusement area known as Piney Beach. Built as part of the 1907 Jamestown Exposition, Piney Beach had a circle swing, train ride, ferris wheel, carousel, and the requisite coaster.

On a typically busy day for employees of the Old Dominion Line in the 1920s, the pier (140) is alive with passengers and their horses and wagons, and with fishermen hoping for a bite. One boat remains to be unloaded and the green cargo added to the neat stack (141), just as soon as the photographer gets his shot, on a summer day in about 1918. Evidence that the workers of a successful oyster packing plant have not been idle (142) looms large in this card from about the same year.

200,000 Bushels of Oyster Shells, Hampton, Va.

142

UNLOADING WATERMELONS, PIER "A," NEWPORT NEWS, VA.

141

Norfolk

Passengers traveling on the Old Bay Line's overnight steamer from Baltimore arrived at Norfolk's Main Street pier with time to spare for a hearty breakfast before leaving the vessel to pursue their day's activities. Some made the trip to conduct business while others journeyed down the Bay to do some sightseeing in the area. The steamer and its crew spent the day going around the harbor unloading and taking on freight of various descriptions before returning to the Main Street pier prior to the northward trip to Baltimore.

Norfolk's founding dates to 1682, when fifty acres of land were purchased from Nicholas Wise for ten thousand pounds of tobacco. In 1705 the House of Burgesses named the new community for Norfolk County in England. By 1736 the region's oldest city became a borough, which allowed it to send a representative to the House of Burgesses. On February 13, 1845, by an act of the General Assembly, Norfolk became a city. Life prospered in the area until 1855, when a yellow fever epidemic wiped out ten percent of the population. Prosperity did not return until after the Civil War, when steamships began calling regularly at the port and a new rail line linked the city with distant parts of the country.

One of the major events in Norfolk's history took place in 1907, when President Theodore Roosevelt arrived on his yacht, *Mayflower,* to open the Jamestown Exposition, a celebration of the 300th anniversary of the settlement at Jamestown. Twenty-one states built replicas of famous buildings in the mini-city on Sewall's Point. The money-losing festivities lasted seven months. Ten years later the federal government purchased the land for the Norfolk Naval Base. Because of the concentration of military installations in the area,

Water Front View, NORFOLK, Va.

3050.

144

ATLANTIC HOTEL, OCEAN VIEW, VA.

82:-SCENE AT CAVALIER BEACH CLUB. NORFOLK. VA.

47540

Norfolk's population swelled with an influx of military personnel and defense workers during each of the world wars. Many chose to remain as residents following the conflicts, helping Norfolk to become the vibrant city it is today.

Before 1907, postcard senders were sometimes provided with a white strip on which to write a brief message, as it was illegal to do so on the back. That space is untouched on this pristine view of the Old Bay Line pier (143) at the west end of West Main Street. The strip of hotels at Ocean View was also part of Norfolk. At the Atlantic (144) guests in the 1920s were charged $3 or $4 per day, with meals included, or up to $25 for the whole week. At the Cavalier Beach Club (145), fully dressed members dance on the beach to big band swing during World War II. At about the same time, the porch holds several guests and the beach is full of hand-drawn vacationers in front of the Lowe Hotel (146). Many slips are empty in this winter view of the yacht piers (147), postmarked from Norfolk on February 21, 1942.

THE LOWE HOTEL, 270 W. OCEAN VIEW AVE., NORFOLK, VIRGINIA

25:-THE NEW MUNICIPAL YACHT PIERS WHERE YACHTSMEN STOP ON WAY TO SOUTHERN WATERS.

NORFOLK. VA.

46196

Ocean View, Va.

148

Ocean View Hotel and Waterfront, Ocean View, Va.

Ocean View

Vacationers with a passion for sea fishing could find no finer place to cast their lines, in the late nineteenth and early twentieth centuries, than Ocean View, east of Norfolk, overlooking the lower Chesapeake Bay. Whether traveling on one of the steamers from Baltimore or by trolley and ferry from nearby Portsmouth, fishermen of the 1920s often landed several hundred fish in as little as an hour's time. In their brochures the Old Bay Line promoted Ocean View as "truly the sportsman's paradise." The Virginia Ferry Corporation, operators of five huge automobile and passenger ferries on their Grand Circle Tours of the Chesapeake Bay, also noted the excellent fishing at Ocean View, "Norfolk's own shore resort."

The Ocean View of today little resembles the popular resort of the past, when vacationers flocked from up and down the East Coast to stay at Norfolk's Chesapeake Bay beach. Begun in 1855 by the Ocean View Company, the resort eventually grew to include hotels such as the Nansemond, with its restful sun parlor, pavilions, cottages, and the Ocean View Amusement Park. In winter or summer the green-and-white striped rooftops of the casino and other concessions gave Ocean View a holiday air.

Families traveling to the beach found mile after mile of beautiful white sand. Patrons loung-

Artfully printed and embossed shells (148) form a neat border for this early view of the bandstand and park at Ocean View in a 1908 card. By 1920 (149) visitors to the ocean seem content to stand at the water's edge in street clothes. In this 1906 beach scene (150) no one goes topless.

150

3015—Bathing Scene at Ocean View, Va.

ing in their deck chairs looked out to the Bay, Capes Henry and Charles, and the Atlantic Ocean. Until it finally closed in 1978, the amusement park never failed to thrill visitors with its succession of roller coasters, beginning with the Figure 8. In addition there were seaplane rides in the 1920s, dancing in the pavilions, a casino that later became the fun house, the Circle Swing, and Kiddyland for the children. If a family forgot to pack the bathing suits, they could rent them at the bathhouse. Ice cream cones, one of the popular refreshments at the park, could be purchased at Doumar's Ice Cream Stand, which opened at Ocean View during the 1907 Jamestown Exposition, three years after Doumar introduced the icy sweet treat at the 1904 St. Louis World's Fair.

Norfolk annexed Ocean View in 1923, absorbing its resort community into the ever-expanding city. The park continued to attract enormous crowds in the years following World War II, and even survived a devastating fire in the late 1950s. Following its demolition in the late 1970s the park returned to life as a quieter Ocean View Beach Park, a beach that attracts people who prefer not to travel all the way to the ocean for a day of fun in the sun.

Ocean View, Summer Resort, near Norfolk, Va.

Pavilion and Boardwalk, Ocean View, Va.

Ocean View Bath Houses, Norfolk, Va.—15

Shade is the place to enjoy the band concert early on a summer evening in this card (151) postmarked from Ocean View on August 4, 1914. Seven years later, the sender of this card (152) noted that his party was "met by M. Simpson with his Buick Six. Wasn't that politeness?" The bathhouse is crowded in this view (153) from about the same time. In 1907 this view of the Circle Swing (154) was addressed to "my blessed brown eyed girlie." Perhaps this 1920s view of Kiddyland (155) best explains why Ocean View was called "The Coney Island of the South."

154

Circle Swing, Ocean View, Va.

155

"KIDDYLAND", OCEAN VIEW, NORFOLK, VA.

PHOTO COURTESY NORFOLK-PORTSMOUTH ADVERTISING BOARD

OA4067

Cape Henry

As steamers traveled down the Bay to Norfolk, passengers eagerly planned their sightseeing trips. One of the favorite points of interest, especially for students of early American history, was Cape Henry. This sandy headland marks not only the southern boundary of the entrance to the Chesapeake Bay but also the first landing site of permanent English settlers in America.

On April 26, 1607, after a harrowing four-month journey across the Atlantic Ocean, a party of 104 men arrived on three tiny ships—the *Sara Constant,* the *Goodspeed,* and the *Discovery.* After exploring the lower reaches of the Bay, the men returned to the cape to erect a large wooden cross, thereby marking their landing spot. The group, grateful to have survived the ocean crossing, named the sandy point Cape Henry, in honor of one of the sons of King James I. They then ventured deeper into Virginia, to fulfill their mission of finding a safe place for a colony, and established Jamestown.

On September 5, 1781, during what became known as the Battle of the Capes, the French fleet, under Admiral Comte deGrasse, engaged the British naval force, which had been sent to reinforce Cornwallis at Yorktown. The conflict blocked the British from fulfilling their role and eventually led to Cornwallis's surrender to General Washington's army in October 1781.

Because of the increasing number of ships passing in and out of the Chesapeake Bay, safe navigation was essential. Unfortunately, the various parties involved failed to agree on the need for a lighthouse. Consequently bonfires guided vessels through the treacherous waters while Maryland, Virginia, the British government, Lord Baltimore, and the British mercantile companies

THE OLD AND NEW LIGHTHOUSE, BY NIGHT, CAPE HENRY, VA.

52228

156   157

Sliding and Climbing Sandhills, Cape Henry, near Norfolk, Va.

The Casino and dancing Pavilion, Cape Henry, Virginia

ROASTING OYSTERS AT THE CASINO, CAPE HENRY, VA.

33062

argued. In late 1789 the Virginia General Assembly, unable to fund the construction of a lighthouse, made the land available to the new federal government. Alexander Hamilton selected John McComb, Jr., of New York as designer. George Washington approved the proposal as America's first federal works project in 1791, and in late October 1792 the fish-oil lamps were lighted, providing a much-needed guide to mariners seeking passage through the capes to Hampton Roads and up the Bay to Baltimore.

During the Civil War, Confederate troops damaged the Cape Henry Light, hoping to make it useless as a guide to their enemies, but Union troops repaired the light and returned it to service. In 1872 during a routine inspection, large cracks were discovered in six of the eight faces, prompting questions about the lighthouse's stability. Some pushed for immediate closure. Instead, money for a new structure was appropriated in 1878, and on December 15, 1881, the keeper lighted the lantern in the new Cape Henry Light, built 350 feet southeast of the old tower.

Although old lighthouses were usually demolished, Old Cape Henry Light, now part of the Fort Story army base, remains as a day marker and popular vantage point for views of the Chesapeake Bay.

The octagonal colonial-era lighthouse is dark, but its nineteenth-century neighbor shines its powerful beam (156) in this imaginatively painted night scene from the 1920s. Before there were man-made diversions, visitors apparently enjoyed scrambling to the top of these dunes (157) to see the ships passing, and then sliding down again. In this 1908 card (158), the Casino appears to be the only building on the otherwise undeveloped beach. By the 1920s the establishment was noted for its famous Lynnhaven oysters (159).

Cape Charles

*"You'll hate to return to your car
on the lower deck
when the ship you're on reaches the other shore!
This crossing of the Chesapeake Bay
is one of the most appreciated, thrilling, yet
restful parts of the Grand Circle Tours.
Don't miss it!"*

Ships of the Virginia Ferry Corporation regularly sailed between Kiptopeke Beach on Cape Charles and their Little Creek port in Norfolk, taking visitors with or without automobiles to see the sights of the lower Chesapeake Bay. Their passengers were urged to breathe the tangy, clean salt air while they sat in comfort or strolled the decks of one of the line's five ships, watching sea birds in flight or the passing ships.

Cape Charles, named in 1607 for the second son of King James I, marks the northern boundary of the entrance to the Chesapeake Bay. Capt. John Smith and his party explored this section of the Eastern Shore in 1608 and met the friendly Indians of the Accomack tribe.

The town of Cape Charles, located on the Bay side a few miles north of the point, dates to 1884, when the New York, Philadelphia and Norfolk Railroad established its southern terminus there after extending its line southward through the peninsula. Steamships regularly called at Cape Charles to carry passengers and freight across the Bay to Norfolk. The railroad brought growth and prosperity to the town, and railroad executives built many of its fine Victorian homes. The broad expanse of white sandy beach stretching to the

HARBOR AT NIGHT, CAPE CHARLES, VA.

25197

161

NK-28—S. S. "Princess Anne" Ferry Boat between Cape Charles and Norfolk, Va.

6A-H2151

CHANNEL BASS — WATER SPORTS AT CAPE CHARLES, VA.

south easily attracted vacationers, while the excellent deep-sea fishing lured sportsmen to this quiet resort.

Placed on the National Register of Historic Places in 1991, Cape Charles continues as a railroad town, serving as the headquarters for the Eastern Shore Railroad, which operates a unique twenty-six-mile rail-barge ferry link to Norfolk.

163

The S. S. Del-Mar-Va., Norfolk, Va.

The moon is just slightly off-center and glows a golden yellow over this peaceful 1920s view of the Cape Charles harbor (160). Brand new and streamlined, the Virginia Ferry Corporation's Princess Anne (161) sails against a typically colored sunset in 1936. In an all-too-common scene from around 1950, two successful fishermen display their trophies (162) at the end of a day on the water. Smaller and three years older than the Princess Anne, the Del-Mar-Va (163) departs on her regular run to Little Creek in this linen card from 1933.

ABOUT THE POSTCARDS

No.	Title	Publisher & Number	Remarks	Date
1	Boaters w/Fish & Shell Border	Unknown	E, PM	1909
2	Going Crabbing	Cochrane & Co., R-23737		c1912
3	Steamer Dreamland at Love Point	J. Thomas Smith, Baltimore, #170	PM	1910
4	Greetings from Betterton	Harry P. Cann & Bro. Co., Baltimore		1951
5	Comic Bathers	Unknown, Ser. 526 No. 2902	E	c1910
6	Greetings from Tilghman Md.	Th. E. L., Series 950	PM	1907
7	Souvenir from Carsons Run	A.S.B., #303	E, PM	1909
8	Steamer Louise, Moonlight	I. & M. Ottenheimer, Baltimore, R37574		c1912
9	Steamer Dreamland	Smith	PM	1911
10	View of Harbor, Baltimore	Ottenheimer, R63627		c1920
11	Old Bay Line Pier, Baltimore	Loritz Bros., Baltimore		c1909
12	Old Bay Line Multi-View	Unknown	PM	1928
13	Dancing on Board	Unknown		c1928
14	Steamers City of Baltimore and City of Norfolk Sister Ships	Curt Teich & Co., Chicago, #719-30		c1930
15	On Shipboard– Merchants & Miners	Unknown	PM	1938
16	Steamer Express	Ottenheimer, #107110	HD	1932
17	Wilson Line Steamer–S.S. Dixie	Teich #7A-H1448		1937
18	8–S.S. Bay Belle	Cann, CT#1B-H378		1941
19	Wagon Bridge, Chesapeake City	Unknown		c1912
20	Steamer Clio at Fair View	Smith		c1910
21	Will you come to Fair View	Unknown #628	PM	1917
22	Excursion Crowd at Car Station	Ottenheimer, R-34858	PM	1915
23	Carousel, Bay Shore Park	Ottenheimer, R-34857	PM	1913
24	Dining Hall, Bay Shore Park	Rinn Publ. Co., #619	PM	1916
25	The Pier at Bay Shore	Ottenheimer, #34856	PM	1913
26	Emma Giles at Tolchester Wharf	Louis Kaufmann & Sons, Baltimore, #A-65298	PM	1924
27	Annapolis from Eastport	George W. Jones, Annapolis, #D 3779		c1910
28	Annapolis, Md.	The Albertype Co., Brooklyn, NY	HC	c1915
29	The Last Farewells	Kaufmann, R-44532	PM	1922
30	Dress Parade, U.S. Naval Academy	George J. Davis, CT#1A3129-N		c1930
31	Midshipmen Preparing for Sailboat Drill	Davis, CT#1B-H2267		1941
32	Midshipmen Sailboat Drill	Davis, CT#1B-H2268	PM	1941
33	Carvel Hall Hotel	Kaufmann, #A-65300	HD	1928
34	General View of Harbor, by Night	Kaufmann, #A-44524		c1920
35	The Baur House and Beach	Albertype	HC	c1930
36	Baur's Beach, Bay Ridge	Teich, #8A-H227	PM	1938
37	Dramatic Activities	Artvue Post Card Co., NY		c1945
38	Our Tents	Artvue		c1945
39	A Cook-Out	Artvue		c1945
40	Sailing	Artvue		c1945
41	Greetings from Beverley Beach	Teich, #9A-H2237		1939
42	Beverley Beach	Teich, #D-5349		c1950
43	Refreshing	Teich, #C-1208	PM	1946
44	Pavilion, Pier and Crab House	Albertype		c1945
45	The Board Walk, Chesapeake Beach	Wm. H. Tutty, #D13777	PM	1912
46	Visitors at Chesapeake Beach	Tutty, #D5140		c1910
47	Just Arrived at Chesapeake Beach	Tutty		1912
48	Crabbing and Fishing	Tutty	PM	1909
49	"Just a Company"	Tutty		c1909
50	Catching the Blues	Cann, #37264		c1930
51	Fishing Boats	Cann, CT#3B-H277		1943
52	Evans Moving Picture	Cann, CT#3B-H275		1943
53	Bowen's Inn	Teich, #1B-H1917		1941
54	Diving Practice, Camp Calvert	Artvue		c1945
55	Canoeing on Breton Bay	Artvue		c1945
56	I'm Just Getting the Feel of Things	Tichnor Bros., Boston	PM	1953
57	The Way We Catch Them Here	Unknown, #247	PM	1940
58	Did 'ya Catch Anything Else?	Tichnor	PM	1961
59	I Had a Beautiful Dream	Tichnor	PM	1953
60	I Could Only Show the Tail	Tichnor		c1943
61	Boy! This is Sumpin'	Tichnor	PM	1943
62	Point Concord Light House	Kaufmann, CT#A-44125		c1915
63	The Outlet Lock	The Rotograph Co., N.Y.C., #53096		c1908
64	Duck Shooting	Kaufmann, CT#R-25633	PM	1925
65	Hotel Bayou	Kaufmann, CT#94541	PM	1928
66	Red Point Beach	Artvue		c1950
67	Red Point Beach	Artvue		c1950
68	McDaniels Yacht Basin	Cann, CT#1B-H2172		1941
69	Pier at Bay Boat Works	Cann, CT#1B-H2173		1941
70	Beach Parties, White Crystal Beach	Mayrose Co., NY		c1950
71	On the Sands	Mayrose		c1950
72	The Nightly Dance	Mayrose		c1950
73	Overlooking the Bay	Mayrose		c1950
74	Cottagers Enjoying the Beach	Mayrose		c1950
75	Some Fun Riding the Waves	Harry C. Meyer, Ocean City, NJ #11480N		c1940
76	I See Your Back	Real Photo	PM	1935
77	Steamer Susquehanna	Owens & Co., Betterton, #197992	PM	1910
78	Bathing Scene at Betterton	Unknown		c1910
79	Betterton Boardwalk	The Chessler Co., Baltimore, #3437	PM	c1925

#	Title	Publisher/Printer	Notes	Date
80	Sassafras Avenue	Owen & Co.	PM	1937
81	Business Section	Kaufmann		c1925
82	The Pier and Amusement Center	Cann, CT#6B-H2056		1946
83	Hotel Betterton	Cann, CT#6B-H2059		1946
84	Hotel Chesapeake	Cann, CT#0C-H337		1950
85	New Arch Entrance	Ottenheimer, #A-38704	PM	1920
86	The Beach, Tolchester	Rinn, #26	PM	1910
87	Steamer Louise Landing	Ottenheimer, #A-38705	PM	1915
88	Excursionists' Luncheon	Tolchester News Co.	PM	1910
89	Whirl-Pool Dips	Chessler, #1211	PM	1915
90	Miniature Train	Chessler, #1210		c1915
91	TB-5 - Miniature Railway	Cann, CT#5B-H1095		1945
92	TB-8 - Steamer Tolchester	Cann, CT#8B-H1487		1948
93	Steamer Tolchester	Ottenheimer, CT#4A-H1820		1934
94	Steamer B. S. Ford	Kaufmann, #52167	PM	1923
95	View of Harbor and Jettie	Cann, CT#5B-H1108	PM	1945
96	Main Street Looking South	Cann, CT#5B-H1109		1945
97	Harbor and Railway	Cann, CT#5B-1107		1945
98	B. C. & A. Wharf, Claiborne	H. C. Monroe, McDaniel, MD, #44327		1911
99	Claiborne, Md.	H. C. Dodson, Jr., St. Michaels, #34754	PM	1911
100	Regatta at Claiborne	Albertype	HC, PM	1909
101	The John M. Dennis	Teich, #1973-30		c1930
102	Scene Near St. Michaels	Unknown	PM	1912
103	St. Michaels, Md. Thoroughfare	Thomas H. Sewell, #659	PM	1909
104	Dreamland	Sewell	PM	1909
105	The Bridge	Dodson	PM	1909
106	The Magic	Mayrose		c1956
107	Waterfront, Oakwood Inn	Mayrose		c1956
108	Beneath the Showers	Mayrose		c1956
109	Main Street	Mayrose		c1956
110	The Pasadena	Associated Litho, Des Moines, Iowa		c1960
111	Air View	Teich, #1B-H1107		1941
112	The Anchorage	Albertype	HC	c1909
113	Music Hall, Plaza	Kaufmann, CT#A-71061		c1925
114	Ratcliffe Manor	Albertype	HC	c1910
115	Hotel Avon	Tichnor, #127645	PM	1935
116	Queen Anne Hotel	Kaufmann, CT#A-71059		c1925
117	Hope House	Teich, #7A359		1937
118	B. C. & A. Steamboat Wharf	Albertype	HC	c1910
119	Oxford Regatta	Albertype	HC	1909
120	Yachts at Anchor	Albertype	HC	c1910
121	Public Square	E. C. Kropp Co., Milwaukee	PM	1912
122	Tred Avon Yacht Club	The Collotype Co., Elizabeth, NJ and New York	HD	1943
123	Morris Street	Albertype	HC	c1925
124	Two Recently Finished Buildings	Mayrose	PM	1947
125	The Harbor	Hoge & Holder, Cambridge	PM	1926
126	B. C. & A. Steamer Talbot	Kaufmann, CT#A–48665	PM	c1925
127	Watching the Boat Races	Kaufmann, CT#R-22926		c1925
128	Hotel Dixon	Kaufmann, CT#R-44925		c1925
129	7–Oakley Beach Hotel	Cann, CT#5B-H1104	PM	1945
130	High Street	Kaufmann, CT#A-4660	PM	1916
131	Yacht Club, Cambridge	Lucas & Fowler, Cambridge Tichnor #72406	PM	1938
132	Waterview Beach Hotel	J. T. Wilson, AD-Items, Delmar, DE, Tichnor #K7114		c1940
133	Boat Landing	Cann, CT#0B-H810		1940
134	Hotel Chamberlin	Unknown		c1910
135	Boat Landing	Kaufmann, CT#122882	PM	c1925
136	Old Point Light	Kaufmann, CT#A-75718		c1925
137	Sherwood Inn	Albertype	PM	1908
138	Hampton Roads	Hugh C. Leighton Co., Portland, Me. #30050		c1908
139	Hampton Roads, Pine Beach Pier	Souvenir P. C. Co., NY, #3014	UB	c1906
140	Old Dominion Pier	Kaufmann, CT#A-75893		c1925
141	Unloading Watermelons	Kaufmann, CT#A-36268	PM	1916
142	200,000 Bushels of Oyster Shells	Cann, #6650		c1920
143	Water Front View, Norfolk	A. C. Bosselman & Co., NY, #3050	UB	c1906
144	Atlantic Hotel	Tichnor, #134524		c1925
145	Scene at Cavalier Beach	Frank G. Ennis, Norfolk, #47540		c1940
146	The Lowe Hotel	Ennis, #49719		c1945
147	The New Municipal Piers	Ennis, #46196	PM	1942
148	Ocean View, Va.	S. Langsdorf & Co., NY	PM, E	1908
149	Ocean View Hotel	Chessler & Oberender, #4024		c1916
150	Bathing Scene	Unknown, #3015	UB	c1906
151	Ocean View, Summer Resort	Unknown, #A-7710	PM	1913
152	Pavilion and Boardwalk	Chessler, #9515	PM	1920
153	Ocean View Bath Houses	Kropp, #28582N		c1922
154	Circle Swing	C. E. Wheelock & Co., Peoria, Ill., #466	PM	1907
155	"Kiddyland"	Kaufmann, CT#0A4067		1920
156	The Old and New Lighthouse	Kaufmann, CT#52228		c1920
157	Sliding and Climbing Sandhills	Cann		c1915
158	The Casino	American News Co., NY, #C1758	PM	1908
159	Roasting Oysters	Kaufmann, CT#33062		c1918
160	Harbor at Night	Savage & Blasingame, Cape Charles, CT#25197		c1918
161	NK-28 - S. S. Princess Anne	Cann, CT#6A-H2151		1936
162	Channel Bass	Mayrose		c1950
163	The S. S. Del-Mar-Va	Tichnor, #78381		1934
164	Greetings from Betterton	Teich Sailboat Scenes, #S–453	PM	1946

Key: c-circa; CT-Curt Teich; HC-hand colored; HD-hand dated; PM-postmarked; UB-undivided back; E-embossed.

S-453

GREETINGS FROM BETTERTON, MD.

© CURT TEICH & CO., INC.

ABOUT THE AUTHORS

Bert Smith is a graphic designer who has worked in print and television for more than thirty years. He teaches in the School of Communications Design at the University of Baltimore, from which he received an M.A. in 1985. After graduating from Baltimore City College and serving for three years in the U.S. Marine Corps, he earned a B.F.A. from the Maryland Institute, College of Art and designed the first television newsgraphics for the Baltimore market at WJZ-TV from 1974 to 1976. Mr. Smith's illustrations, design, and typography have won awards from the New York Art Director's Club, *Print* Magazine, the American Institute of Graphic Arts, *Graphic Design:USA,* and the Printing Industries of America. His other collections of vintage postcards, *Greetings from Baltimore* and *Down the Ocean,* are also published by the Johns Hopkins University Press.

Anthea Smith is an award-winning painter and the author of *Finding the Charm in Charm City,* with photographs by Huguette May. Her early professional experiences included work as a graphic artist, a production manager, and the vice president of an advertising agency in Baltimore. She also attended the Maryland Institute, College of Art, earning a Certificate in Fine Arts in Painting in 1987. She and her husband live in the historic mill village of Hampden in Baltimore.

Racing, Fishing, Boating, Gunning, Indoor Pool, Dancing, Rail, Motor and Boat facilities. Midway between Washington and New York. Garage.

POST CARD

THIS SPACE FOR ADDRESS ONLY.

2 CENTS

HAVRE DE GRACE MD.
MAY 14
11 A.M.
1928

B. C. & A. STEAMER TALBOT AT WHARF, CAMBRIDGE, MD.

Cambridge is blessed with excellent railroad and steamboat facilities. Here is shown one of the palatial night steamers plying between Baltimore and Cambridge.

POST CARD

CAMBRIDGE, MD.
OCT 13
6-PM
1950

UNITED STATES POSTAGE
1 CENT 1
GEORGE WASHINGTON

THIS SPACE FOR ADDRESS ONLY.

POST CARD

SEP 7
AM
190_

COMMEMORATIVE SERIES 1907
POSTAGE ONE CENT

Miss Louise Arrie +
#42. Ol.

CLAIBO___
POST CARD
MD.
UNITED STATES
1 CENT

Mrs. Cora Oberholtzer

Bechtelsville

Pa.

This place is 5 miles from us, there is water all around us. have not gone bathing yet but have been fishing one boat last night had caught a large fish & had 2 bites but party caught 14. we will go see them pick crab meat this morning they say its very interesting. very large farm all around here. we surely will like.

ST. MICHAELS PHARMACY, ST. MICHAELS, MD.
PUBLISHED FOR QUALITY—The Albertype Co., Brooklyn, N.

CARD

OLD POINT COMFORT, VA.
JAN 23
3½ PM
1908

This space is for the Address only

This space may be used for Correspondence

Mr. Henry Derby
310. Academy St.
Jersey City
New Jers

BALTIMORE STEAM PACKET CO.
(OLD BAY LINE)
The Oldest Line   The Newest Boats
The Best Service
BETWEEN
BALTIMORE   NORFOLK   OLD POINT
AND PORTSMOUTH, VA.

On Board New Steamer "State of Virginia"

____est Grandmother
I think I'm falling
in love. I just saw
the skipper — & o.
I am having a
wonderful time.
Love

Post Card
THIS SPACE FOR ADDRESS ONLY
1928
UNITED STATES
2 CENTS

Mrs. Ida J. Bosser
1317 State Stre
Harrisburg,
Penn

BAY SHORE SERIES

POST CARD

SPARROWS POINT
MD.
10 AM

U.S. POSTAGE
ONE CENT

THIS SIDE FOR CORRESPONDENCE

THE ADDRESS TO BE WRITTEN ON THIS SIDE

Mr Jacob Marr